Other books by James Cahill

Fiction:

Lost in the Slipstream

Love to Turn You On

Solving the mystery of female sexuality; two men in a candid conversation about women

James Cahill

ISBN: 1480015547
ISBN-13: 9781480015548

"The more girls a boy has, the better. He has a bright look, having reaped the fruits, blooming. He stalks, sure-shouldered, and you have the feeling he's got more in him, a fatter heart, more stories to tell. For a girl, with each boy, it's as though a petal gets plucked each time."

Writer, Susan Minot
Fiction: Lust

"They get what they want, and they never want it again."

Singer/songwriter, Courtney Love
Song: Violet

"A woman looks to one man to meet all of her needs; a man looks to all women to meet one of his needs."

Documentary
Human Sexuality

"Such a fuss was made of sex, and then, finally, it was a let down. Vastly overrated. Marriage and commitment seemed the death of any erotic life. No one I knew spoke of his or her great love life. I certainly didn't. I muddled along, making love the best I could, defending my ineptitude as well as I able.

One day, all of this changed.

An event occurred that would alter, forever, not only the way I made love to a woman, but that caused a complete upheaval in the way I thought about them. I had been failing women over and over - I realized this only later. But after this particular incident, I finally understood what women are talking about when they say men are not meeting their needs."

Dear Reader,

I wish I had this book in my twenties. This is a tale of a journey and a discovery. If you're a heterosexual male in your twenties, and you have this book, well, I envy you, because with a bit of thoughtful practice, you can open the door to a possible lifetime of great lovemaking and thrilled women in your future. If you're older, no problem, it's never too late to have a wonderful sex life. For women, this could be an excellent 'conversation starter' with a partner. Personally, I was staggered at how little I knew about being intimate with a woman – and probably, how little most men know - until I learned what good lovemaking really looks like.

I know that people often read books like this in the same way that they engage in bad sex: they want to skip ahead to the good parts. To understand the concepts, you really need to read this as the journey in which it is written - in order. Please begin with page one, then go to page two, then three, and so on. Only then will a picture emerge of how women tend to think about intimacy, and how this underpins what it means to be a truly amazing lover. And men, don't be surprised if you experience a sea change - in the way that you think about women, in the way that you make love to them, and best of all, in a female partner who becomes fabulously enthusiastic about making love to you.

Best of luck on your journey.

Sincerely,

James Cahill

Love to Turn You On

Just recently, I received a call from an old friend.

I had known Tony since kindergarten, and despite a few intermittent gaps when he was off backpacking in Asia, Africa, or some other exotic locale I'd never get to, we had maintained a consistent, dependable, and tolerably close friendship since. He desired a chat, he said with a customary animation that always seemed to perk me up; a chat with me alone which was of paramount importance.

In truth, when he called, I was buried. A stack of exams to grade, my daughter Julie's soccer game to root for, and this evening, my wife Cindy and I had planned a long overdue evening of drinks at the Bluestein's - it wasn't often we got to hear about Joe's latest real estate coup - but Tony was insistent.

Fine, I told him, I'd look forward to it. I always did.

I don't want to say much about Tony beyond what he wishes revealed here, which frankly, is precious little. The following is an account of my meeting with him, and though it is a record of that evening as best as I could render it, Tony insisted that he wanted no part of it, adding that as a budding deconstructionist I would understand.

Budding, my ass, I told him. You're completely irrelevant.

He thanked me.

James Cahill

And what did Tony wish revealed? That, in his words, he would trust to my own, uncanny discretion. Canny or not, I will say a few things: In a world where people lapsed into careers, barbecues, lawn mowing, Sunday papers and the somnambulism necessary to bear such oppression, Tony was unique. This isn't to say he was flaky, quirky or endearingly eccentric. No ponytail, no earring, and long as I'd known him, catless. He was neither rebel, bohemian, or some reckless, indulgent romantic, and the one black t-shirt he owned granted him little in the way of tortured-poet chic. I could go on about what he was not, but simply put, he just seemed quietly vigilant against a life of second choices. He lived this way - and I wish to be clear on this point - not out of some obstinate philosophical pose, but rather, because he simply didn't have a choice.

In the comments section of his grade school report cards, Tony's teachers always wrote: "Only does what interests him." He simply could not engage in a task he found boring. Boredom caused him pain. Actual, physical pain. I had seen Tony, as an adult, in earshot of some tedious, pontificating windbag, holding his head in agony as if each bromide impaled his skull like a hot dagger. More often, he lapsed into a state of deep daydreaming. 'Earth to Tony,' was a phrase painfully familiar, and more than once I saw him wince at the smartass who uttered it.

Only much later did he begin to accept this aspect of himself, but even as early as fourth grade, I gasped as I watched him shove aside a page of long division without a care. He did this not because he was lazy. Not because he couldn't do the problems. Tony could multiply and divide with the best of us. Long division was dull and therefore unbearable. He was sent to the corner, but this punishment was wasted on him, because there, he could lapse into a sweet, private, inner excursion to some secret place infinitely more fascinating.

In college his daydreaming became chronic. Though he did well in a few courses, or rather, with professors who were gifted lecturers, for the most part he could hardly attend to a word that was said. Even when a teacher was particularly stimulating, or if the man or women behind the podium uttered some sudden, stunning bit of wisdom, Tony was instantly gone, pursuing, within the privacy of his own mind, this new and riveting notion as the lecture moved on to other topics that would find no place in his note-taking. A course that mandated discussion was, consequently, a nightmare. If called upon to speak, he had no idea what was being discussed, any recollection of what had already been said on the topic, or even the slightest notion of the question itself, and often he turned crimson with embarrassment. But when asked to make an oral presentation, this normally quiet young man would stun everyone, teacher and student alike. In classes we shared, I sat back and grinned at the pleasant shock on every face in the room when Tony spoke, not only with dazzling fluency, not only with a contagious fascination for his topic, but with poise, assurance, and charm. Still, his grades suffered. His girlfriend, headed for a degree in special ed., offered her diagnosis: Tony had a textbook attention problem.

"You have a future," he told her.

She blushed.

Needless to say, grad school held no attraction for him. He would miss it all or slit his throat in pure frustration in trying not to miss it. And if Tony did, say, complete a doctorate, and thus, the rest of his life was confined to working in one, narrow area, I'm certain the claustrophobia would cast him into an abyss of depression.

But when he was interested! This was something else altogether. When a subject grabbed him, Tony became obsessed. He probed, tortured, twisted it in ways no one else seemed to consider. He loved asking questions - he couldn't stop himself - and though it was hardly his intent, people often felt on trial around him. He just wanted to reach the center of something or someone, and frankly, I think it was the sleepwalking crowd who hated his questions the most. When he suspected that someone felt unjustly interrogated, he immediately asked, 'do you mind if I keep asking?' If the response was, "Go ahead," I believe he felt, not only relief, not only gratitude, but also a profound affection for the person.

When asked to describe someone, we usually begin, for some reason, with his or her job. Since I had known Tony, I've developed a rule about asking what people do for a living: I don't. There have been enough times in his life - and some in mine - when circumstances had him supporting himself with a job that, frankly, was embarrassing. I felt bad for him, particularly when he could have mopped the floor with most of the folks in my graduate program. People ask, "What do you do?" and as you tell them, they bob their head a few times, sum you up in a way that has no connection with who you are, then retreat back into land of nod.

For those unique individuals who take the big risk, who pursue what fascinates them, often their job won't speak about them in any way that matters. But lucky you, if the flame that burns brightest in your soul is something you can major in and collect a paycheck for. Or, through cleverness and diligence, you can arrange the world to suit your own uniqueness rather than twisting yourself into a pretzel to suit the world. To contort, to compromise, for Tony, would be to join the walking dead. I don't believe he ever actually thought about it, but if he did, he might say this: if a sparkling inner life resides within you, let that make its own statement, for those interested and perceptive enough to see it. Personally, I don't even like to tell people I teach English, or at what University. How many times have I suffered the comment, "Better watch my grammar!" or laughed politely at some joke about my red pen.

I don't use a red pen, and I hate laughing politely.

So we will leave Tony's job out of this. It will be a small mystery. Irrelevant, soon forgotten.

Well then, what are his credentials? If he has something to say, why should anyone listen?

I will answer this very good question with a brief anecdote.

As teenagers, Tony and I joined our friend Kam who owned a van and we all went camping over Spring break at San Clemente State Beach. Kam had some old bikes in his garage that we brought along, and we spent one electrifying afternoon riding at breathtaking speeds down the long and steep T street hill. We went down once, pushed the bikes back to the top, then flew down again, each time, using the brakes less and less, going faster and faster, achieving velocities that would render manhood irrefutable. At the bottom of the hill, the road turned sharply right and left - like a T - and we squeezed our hand breaks and slowed to a stop to avoid crashing into the chain link fence that stretched across the far side of the road. To turn at the ungodly speeds we had attained was impossible. And the bikes, as I said, were old; they had been decomposing in Kam's garage for quite some time. Tony, polite as always and last to choose, ended up with the worst of the three. It had one brake only - the front - and plenty of rust. And it was big. This bike had belonged to Kam's much taller older brother Jack, who was now playing power forward on a partial scholarship at a small college in the mid-west.

Twice, we flew down the hill.

Twice, we slowed to safety before reaching the fence.

The third trip down we pedaled with particular ferocity, bent on settling the question of manhood for a lifetime. Just beyond mid-way and roughly ten feet off to my left, Tony squeezed his single hand break. It gripped the front wheel, briefly. With a sharp, metallic ripping sound, the break tore loose from the frame, flipped up and away, then dangled from the cable.

Tony uttered a single obscenity. He spoke the word clearly, but not in the expected, shouted sense of pure terror. Tony's expletive was more high-pitched, in the range of astonishment, of fascination. And there he was, careening down the long and steep T street hill with no perceivable way to stop. We glanced briefly at each other. The air whizzed around our ears, over our sunburned arms and legs. The concrete blurred with ragged-toothed cruelty below. The wire mesh fence rose up closer by the second. And here was Tony, brakeless, gaining velocity, sorting through his options. What were they? Take his chances with the fence? That could mean death or the certainty of becoming a cripple for life. He could he lay the bike down and skid – far and away, the bloodiest option – which, at the very least, would put an end to a track season that was a month from league finals. He wore shorts, a t-shirt and a pair of cheap sandals - you might call them flip-flops. But his feet were much too far from the ground. Even to scoot forward, off the seat, Tony was way too high up to get any kind of purchase on the road. And even then, he'd have all that angry metal between his legs.

Six seconds to impact.

Scraped hideously?

Kiss the fence at top speed?

From my vantage point, laying the bike down seemed his only choice.

Now it was three to five seconds before what could be a life-changing conclusion. Did I witness panic? Hysteria?

Blasting down T street hill, Tony revealed none of these. I tried to guess his immediate future. He would reach the bottom and cross the road in the next instant, but to my astonishment, he delivered a solution I had never considered. Tony stood up on the left pedal, threw his right leg over the bike as if to dismount, then placed his flip-flop hard against the concrete. Smoke rose from the contact. And with this as a brake, he glided elegantly to a stop.

In silent awe, I gripped two healthy hand brakes.

That evening, we sat around the campfire, laughing, retelling the story, passing around his smooth-bottomed flip-flop. Had I been on that bike instead of Tony, the results of a brake popping off at 40 to 50 miles an hour might have been quite different. I can safely say that most of the excellent professors at my university would be arranged, in various attitudes of blood-spattered defeat, across the chain link fence.

I have quite a few other, quite similar Tony stories, but this one will suffice; and, frankly, it will serve as credentials enough for me. When it mattered, his thinking soared.

Tony's inability to do what didn't matter, which he could manage with some finesse as a student, he discovered to be a problem much more daunting in the working world. There, he was not embraced, and this left him prone, often, to black depressions. Which is to say nothing more than that he was real, found rejection painful, and a snug fit in this world he has yet to find. Though not given to self-pity, he wondered aloud once, in the midst of a very difficult period, if perhaps his birth was unplanned, because he felt as though he lacked an invitation to his own life. But he quickly added, *I'm whining*, and asked me to please tell him to shut up. I told him I'd never tell him to shut up, and it occurred to me that this - his very own life - was the one problem he couldn't solve.

And what did he have to tell me?

"I have something I'd like you to write," he said.

"To write?"

I had plenty of my own projects and only so much time to get them done. To ask me to drop everything and write something for him, frankly, was impossible. From anyone else, I would assume a certain impertinence at such a request, but I knew Tony. He was dreamy, certainly, but considerate. Writing, typing; these drove him crazy. Further, he was generous. He rarely asked me for anything, so when he called in a favor, I knew it was important, and though I was not necessarily agreeable, I was always curious.

"A clue," I said.

"Women," he said. "I think I understand them."

I hesitated for a moment.

"You mean you finally-"

"I can't explain this over the phone," he said. "Tell me. In honesty. How's your love life?"

I took a breath. I once asked Tony if he'd ever considered a course in icebreakers. A conversation with Tony never included anything resembling a warm-up. (How could it, when a mere mention of the weather had him gagging?) Actually, I always liked this about him. Almost always. But while his question was reasonable and would get an answer, I needed a moment on a topic I preferred not to broach, not just yet anyway, even with Tony.

"My love life," I said, clearing my throat. I told him I thought it was normal, which was hideously vague, but not altogether dishonest. My lovemaking with Cindy had plummeted since our first year of marriage. The way, I guess, it plummets in all marriages. I leaned my head out the door of my study to make sure my wife wasn't in earshot. "Well, Cindy, you know, I think she has some intimacy issues. But we're working-"

"Intimacy issues."

"Yes," I said, *"intimacy issues."*

"Listen," Tony said. "My God. This is exactly, *exactly* what I want to... it's what *drives* people... James, listen: women aren't happy. They're not happy and men... we don't know how to make them

James Cahill

happy. Lovemaking plummets, men are miserable, then... affairs.
The whole thing is so unbelievably-"

"I haven't had an affair," I said quickly.

"That's fine," he said, with no interest whatsoever. "But this is
it. This is what I want to talk about. How about tomorrow night?
Can you meet me?"

"Tonight would be better," I said, again, glancing around for
my wife.

"Perfect."

I had no idea where this was headed, but I thought, in that
instant, about my marriage. The humiliating coaxing and cajoling.
The sexual double-entendres with an angry edge. And something
recent, and frankly, a bit scary: my wife and I, sleeping who-needs-
you style on opposite sides of the bed. Then, once a week or, at
times, once a month; the grudging, obligation Cindy performed as
my wife.

What *did* women want?

Tony and I made the arrangements.

Before we plunge in, I only wish to add a few items. Though I
did take scanty notes, I have a fairly good memory. I tried my best
to preserve, not only the content, but also Tony's voice throughout
this narrative. When he seemed unable to contain his enthusiasm I
tried to get it down perfectly and use quotations. His thinking tends
toward the digressive and though at times he needed to be gently
reigned in, for the most part, I found it best just to let his mercurial
brain roam at blissful random. Often, what I thought was a digres-
sion headed oddly and neatly back to his main subject. At times he
was repetitive, but this was only with particularly important topics.
And, in this spirit of problem solving, easy conversation, and reader
clarity, we can invent our own narrative devices. So, rather then the
common three dots across the page to begin a new section, when
you encounter: TTT, this means Tony is about to chat in the first
person. If you see: JJJ, that's yours truly, James, about to speak. Any
headings, or slight inclinations toward order are my own, and he
gave me a free hand to tidy up or slash and burn as I saw fit. Mostly,
I left things as they were. It's a topic that I believe benefits endlessly

from a personal voice. I wouldn't want this explained to me, say, by a sexologist or a text. The lecturing condescension of the former would get on my nerves. The disembodied humorlessness of the latter would turn what is certainly the most thrilling subject on earth to talcum powder. Finally - and I say this with all due respect - it cannot be explained to a man by a woman. Women have tried; dear God, have they tried, and for many reasons - and Tony gets to them - it doesn't work. It needs to be explained to men, by a man, in the language of men. It needs to be explained by a man who understands women.

What man can make such a claim? *To understand women.* Tony, I believe, has made a credible stab at this formidable conundrum.

It's true, he has no advanced degree, and therefore, to some, no authority to talk about anything. If an idea worth hearing arrives in a mind that lacks the ambassador of an advanced degree, do we close our ears? Do we wait until some heavily honored authority gives us the same information, larded with citations, bombast, footnotes, and other forms synaptic refrigeration? Do we wait for the expert to tell us how to eat, speak, feed the third world, solve the AIDS crisis, and make love to a woman? If say, some less conspicuous individual has a few worthy thoughts, shouldn't we listen?

Among Tony's gifts is his lack of ego - his honesty in describing his failures, his modesty in describing his successes. Indeed, his self-effacement, his terror - always unfounded - of appearing arrogant was, at times, annoying. But his true forte was problems. From the small, nonsensical to the grand and global. I have heard his thoughts on everything from laser beams and extra-terrestrials as a boy, to the most perfect distance running program, to answers to crime, education, the drug problem, the energy crisis, lower back pain. His solutions, at first glance, had a cockeyed, angular, back door quality, but after some reflection... well, you had to wonder at their possibilities. Tony, of course, lacked any authority to see his ideas fly.

So now his fascination turned to women. I can't even claim, when he called, to be aware of any personal problem with the fairer sex - in fact, I fancied myself, then, quite competent in that particular area - but I was ready to listen. And I want to add, that this

James Cahill

interview, from one man to another, is, by extension and through this writing, to all men. It occurred in a brewpub, at a heavily varnished solid oak table. Please consider yourself a friend, at that table, welcome, with a beer, and listening.

In fact, go ahead: pour yourself a tall, cool one.

Though a small part is for women, this, primarily, is guy territory.

And, personally, I must confess in painful, candid retrospect: my own marriage seemed to be careening down a steep hill; brakeless, and picking up speed.

My encounter with Tony took place over one long evening in a favorite pub in Northern California. We ate burgers and fries.

J J J

Tony asked me to give him my notion of a great lover.

I laughed. I glanced over at the long bar with the Saturday evening crowd lined up on stools, at the grinning, portly, mustachioed bartender, and then at an idle dart board off to the right. I looked at Tony, now sitting across from me. He had the slight build of a distance runner, short dark brown hair, and wore a long-sleeve navy blue t-shirt.

I said, "Pierre."

"Pierre?"

I leaned forward. "I imagine a guy named Pierre. Dark and brooding, one of those intense, pony-tailed artists - a sculptor - living in the Latin Quarter of Paris. He wears tight black pants, a billowing white shirt, and as he hammers and chisels away, he pauses to gaze with white-hot artistic passion at the stone before him. Errant strands of hair escape his ponytail and hang rakishly over his rugged cheekbones. He pounds a bit more, then steps back, looks over his work, nods once, then reaches for Babette, his slim, short-skirted actress lover, and off they go, heading out into the night, to the bohemian haunts of Paris. There, he introduces her to his fascinating, brilliant and eccentric friends - writers, poets, artists, musicians – who laugh and drink late into the evening. Then, back home at well past midnight, he stares into Babette's eyes. And, in a second fit of passion, he carries her to his brass bed where they make sudden, feverish love for hours. In the morning, they awake in a tangle of sheets and limbs. Both look just as gorgeous as they did the night before. His hair falls in his face but in a cool and effortless move, he pulls it back into a windswept ponytail. Then, suddenly, he stares, not at Babette, but at the stone in the center of his studio. The passion ignites in him yet again and he seizes his hammer and chisel, as Babette watches in ardent wonder."

Tony took a breath. "Damn!" he said. "You're good at this. Give me another."

"Another," I said. "I saw this movie: The Bodyguard. The slim and beautiful diva gets attacked onstage by a bunch of frighteningly tough skinheads. She faints into Kevin Costner's arms. Kevin carries her to safety, through a rioting mob, but not before kicking three or four, tattooed and quite vicious-looking punks unconscious. That's it. I watched this scene and felt terrifically inadequate. Personally, I couldn't kick *anyone* unconscious, even if the poor bastard was tied up in front of me. I certainly couldn't do it while carrying a beautiful diva. But I glanced around the theater, at what seemed to me, a sea of wide-eyed females. I read their minds, knew their single, shared thought: *'That's* what I'm looking for!' And this left me even more depressed."

"Please," Tony said with a grin. "This is beyond my wildest - I beg, one more."

"Okay, one more, you bastard, but this is it. James Bond and a fabulously hot, voluptuous babe are tied up in an airplane and surrounded by fifty enemy agents. He frees them both, beats up thirty agents, leaps out of the plane with her in his arms, and they parachute to safety as they watch the plane crash into a cliff. On the ground, James purchases a camel from a passing nomad. They mount the camel, and as they ride off, she puts her arms lovingly around him. And James says, 'I know a restaurant in Baghdad that serves an excellent couscous. I believe we can make it before they close.'"

Tony looked at me. "An *excellent couscous?*" he said. "James, Kevin, and Pierre. Quite a crew. Clearly, men of fabulous competence. But great lovers?"

I shrugged. I had assumed so.

Tony then asked me if I'd ever heard these phrases: "Go slow. Be gentle. Talk to me."

Had he been hiding in my bedroom? I wondered if he'd hidden in every bedroom I'd ever entered since I first had the miraculous luck to unbutton a blouse. He was a good friend. I told him, yes, I'd heard them.

We ordered two pints of Muskrat Skank from a distracted but quite lovely waitress. Before they arrived, Tony leaned in, lowered his voice almost conspiratorially, and spoke.

T　　　T　　　T

I've heard them too, Tony said.

I've heard them suggested, shouted, whispered seductively. I've heard them as reprimands. I've seen disappointment on a woman's face I did not understand. I only knew that I had disappointed my lover in some mysterious way. I felt unmanly and inept. I defended myself vehemently.

Didn't I go slowly? Wasn't I gentle?

But the insidious, painful message? I had failed my woman. In some key, inexplicable way, I had not only failed her, but had revealed myself as an oaf.

An oaf in bed.

The notion was so distasteful I hated to consider it. I would admit my failure to no one.

Instead, I blamed women.

Women! What did they want? This strange need for seemingly endless foreplay! What was the point? Then, almost always, this thoroughly bizarre request: *talk to me*, which truthfully, seemed downright rude. But to discuss any of this was dangerous. Was I alone in my bewilderment? I certainly did not wish to suffer the ridicule of my peers, all of whom, it seemed, said they were either great lovers, or, perhaps if they were more honest, were oafs like myself and struggling valiantly to maintain a pose somewhere between Kevin, James, and Pierre.

Conversations with men.

Friends revealed little of their own experience. Sexual discussions were rarely personal. Though we might comment on the luscious attributes of a waitress and what we might like to do with her, I believe our actual love lives were quite different from the wistful, hypothetical lives we shared. When the honesty came out, most of my friends - married or in long relationships - weren't getting nearly the sex they wanted.

"Once a week, if I'm lucky," Tom said.

"Maybe once a month," Fred confided. "*Maybe.*"

Both said marriage was great except for this. They were happy, they said with weary bobs of their heads that left me unconvinced. Sex was the only real battle. Both agreed vaguely that things changed when you got married. Then Tom admitted that he was going crazy. Fred uttered something obscene, and said, "What's *with* these women?" Tom considered finding a prostitute, but added strangely, "Maybe I'll talk to my wife about it first."

"Talk to your wife about getting a hooker!" Fred laughed. "Good luck!"

Fred then revealed that he had found himself a girlfriend. *Cheat*, he said. It was the only answer to marriage. Marriage, he said philosophically, was designed for women. All men want to have sex with other women.

Tom agreed.

Though I was not married, I adhered, somewhat romantically, to the notion that if you found the right partner the heat would never diminish. But I wasn't sure. "If you found the perfect women," I asked, "You would still want to have sex with other women?"

Both shouted: "*Yes!*"

Many other men, those who were honest enough to share something personal, expressed this same frustration. They blamed the institution of marriage, which vastly favored women, who did not, they felt, have a biological need for constant sex, and to make love to everything in sight, as did men.

My own erotic fortunes were equally abysmal. I was living with my girlfriend, and though I expected this co-habitation to be a final relief from a persistent, lustful agony, which blazed in me like a supernova, in fact, just, the opposite occurred. My girlfriend and I almost never made love. It was our biggest battle.

I confess: like my friends, I was going out of my mind.

Conversations with women.

While men shared precious little, women were infinitely more vocal on the subject. What I gathered from them seemed equally distressing. Though I did not hear opinions on this subject from a great many women, those I spoke with made me privy to conversations they'd had with many female friends. One group of ladies met regularly for tea and discussed everything with abandon. My connection here was a woman named Karen. She told me that most of her female friends said they either didn't like sex at all or were indifferent. Many women said was it a burden. One explained how her husband made love to her once a week, every Saturday morning whether she was in the mood or not. Another told of her husband coming home drunk and how diligently she would pretend to be asleep. Even when he was sober, she hated to make love with him. Another, with little enthusiasm, but at least, with admirable wifely loyalty, said that though she and her husband rarely made love, when they did, "Dave could last an hour."

The women laughed.

They bonded.

I asked Karen about the phrase, 'Go slow, be gentle', wondering whether it ever came up in their conversations.

"Oh, God!" she said. "Go slow, be gentle! It's almost a cliché! That's what all women want from their men!"

I wandered through bookstores, first to the fiction section to see what was new, but then, inevitably, furtively, to the section whose title itself gave me slight blood rush: *Sexuality*. I thumbed among drawings and actual photos of naked couples in contorted positions, tanglings, and acrobatics. Was this what it meant to be a good lover? I tried a few when I had the opportunity. They were mildly fun, briefly interesting, often exhausting, but finally, they seemed to make little difference to my girlfriend or me.

I assumed this was it.

Though women and sex fascinated me endlessly, I found myself, not working on the problem of becoming a better lover, but rather, working on a brilliant verbal defense when a woman seemed disappointed or actually accused me openly of not meeting her needs. I argued because I felt embarrassed and terribly inept. She wanted touching. Didn't I touch her? She asked for it, I did it. In truth, the amount of touching a woman wanted seemed hideously out of line with the demands of my own mood, when the two of us were naked and alone together. Regardless, the discussion never got far and our lovemaking diminished. Men and women; what a mis-match. Was this frosty contentiousness the only answer?

A Big, Big Problem.

Colleen, a friend and an anthropologist who was, by turns, brassy on the one hand and little girl giggly on the other - and endearing in both modes - had much to say on the subject. She, and every one of her female friends and colleagues concurred: they were unsatisfied by sex (with men), and that yes, 'going slow, being gentle' was the problem. She said, basically - and graphically - most men want to 'stick it in' as soon as possible, hammer away as long as they can, and then it's over. This, she said, does little to please a woman.

She said it's a big, big problem.

Based on her experience and conversations with friends, she felt that men, almost universally, don't know how to sexually please women. The problem is so serious that she felt - and she said this, only somewhat tongue in cheek - that men should make love to men and women should make love to women. Men could go off and be as hurried, promiscuous and cavalier about sex as they wanted, and women could be monogamous and patient and experience the greater emotional connection with each other that they needed. She said plenty of research supported the notion that we could all love anyone with equal satisfaction. And, she added, men and women could come together for procreation when necessary, and there were plenty of ways to organize the world, the traditional family being only one.

I admired such outrageous thinking. But, despite the research, I told her, I preferred women. In fact, I wanted to explain this to her. I wanted to give her an intimate glimpse of the inner workings of a male brain. Colleen seemed to be one of the few women who could handle it.

I told her, "I want to have sex with every woman I meet."

"*Really?*"

"Absolutely," I said. I reminded her of a scene from the movie, *When Harry Met Sally.*

Harry: ... no man can be friends with a woman he finds attractive, he always wants to have sex with her.

Sally: So you're saying that a man can be friends with a woman he finds unattractive.

Harry: Nuh, you pretty much wanna nail them too.

Colleen remembered the scene, and asked, "Men, I've read, have a sexual thought every six seconds. Is it true?"

"At least every six seconds. I marvel at the workings of my own mind. I can't even believe what I'm thinking half the time. If all men walked around with a little video screen over their heads that revealed their thoughts - women would be outraged!"

"Really?" she said, and this too, stunned me. Colleen had lived with men her entire life. She had raised two males, married and divorced another. She was a bright, perceptive woman. She was an Anthropologist, a student of humanity! But she didn't understand this basic fact about men, which nearly all men experienced, struggled with and understood. But for that matter, what did I know of women? Could I guess what might be on a similar video screen above their heads?

"Can a woman ever know what it's like to be a man?" I asked her. "There are times when I'd like to have sex with sixteen women in succession, and *I don't even want to know their names!*"

She looked at me, stunned. After a moment, she said, for the third time, *"Really?"*

"Really. And without hating me, please tell me why my mind works this way."

She shrugged.

We're programmed this way. (Colleen says 'programmed socially'; I say 'cosmically hard wired' - in a continuing discussion that has raged over more than one evening of pizza and beer.) A cavalier, constant lust, for the most part, is endemic to male psychology, and we damn well better be silent about it.

J   J   J

Tony was interrupted as the beers arrived, and dear God in Heaven, there's nothing like the first pull off an ice cold Muskrat Skank. He put down his mug and asked again about another famous scene in *When Harry Met Sally*.

"Remember?" he said.

"Of course. Who could forget? When Sally faked the orgasm in the restaurant, to prove to Harry -"

"- that he could never tell if a woman's orgasm was real or fake-"

"I remember."

"Listen to this," Tony said. "I mentioned at work that I'd seen the movie. Of course, the fake orgasm scene came up in our discussion. My boss, a woman, said, 'Every woman I know could relate to that scene.'"

"I was stunned.

"*'Every woman?'*"

"'Every single one,'" she said.

"I thought about this. All the women she knew could relate to it. I asked her: 'So are you saying, they've *all faked orgasms*.'"

"Pretty much," she said. "Every single, solitary-."

"Have *you?*" I asked.

"She smiled and said evasively, 'we could all relate to that scene.'"

"Think about it," Tony said, looking at me. "We're not pleasing our women. They try to tell us how and we don't understand. Or maybe they soft-soap us with a sham of counterfeit climaxing to make us *think* we're pleasing them! How the hell did it get like this?"

"My wife would never fake an orgasm!" I said quickly. "Why would she? Why would I want her to?"

"You'd never know," Tony said with a grin. "Meg Ryan proved it."

"Hmph."

Tony watched me for a moment. "We'll come back to Meg in a minute. Lovely Meg. But the point is, men are not pleasing their women. Listen-"

T   T   T

Of course, I had to ask my friend the anthropologist: "So... Colleen. Have you ever, you know... faked one?"

She glanced around to be sure no one could hear her, then she said, quietly, "Yes." And then she shouted: "*But you have to!*"

Colleen's 'but you have to' is a statement of unending fascination.

It seemed we were at a precarious place in history. The women's movement had taught women they were entitled to an orgasm (or more than one), but it hadn't taught men how to give them one. We couldn't go back to the old ways, where a woman simply satisfied her man, perhaps as tacit compensation for the fact that he went to work, earned money, and fed her. In pre-liberation days, women were silent, dutiful, and men had no need to be good lovers. Today women work, earn money, and feed themselves. A relationship is no longer based on gratitude and service, but equality, and men needed to do better.

We can't go back. Pandora's Box has been opened. Women were trying to tell men what they needed. Were they not explaining it in a way that men could understand? Or were men simply not listening? Or, were we listening, and trying diligently, but failing miserably? Or, based on Meg Ryan's famous scene - to which, apparently, all women could relate - women weren't even trying to tell us. In fact, they were telling us the very opposite - that we were all perfectly wonderful lovers - when in fact, we weren't.

All very confusing.

The Women's Movement, Colleen and I both agreed, was the most astounding event to occur in our lifetimes. Women had burned their bras, taken a step forward. And men had to take a step forward to meet them.

But what were we supposed to do?

An Epiphany.

Such a fuss was made of sex, and then, finally, it was a let down. Vastly overrated. Marriage and commitment seemed the death of any erotic life. No one I knew spoke of his or her great love life. I certainly didn't. I muddled along, making love the best I could, defending my ineptitude as well as I able.

One day, all of this changed.

An event occurred that would alter, forever, not only the way I made love to a woman, but that caused a complete upheaval in the way I thought about them. I had been failing women over and over - I realized this only later. But after this particular incident, which I shall soon explain, I finally understood what women are talking about when they say men are not meeting their needs, and, what a woman means when she says, 'go slow, be gentle'.

The moment itself was not particularly special or dramatic. No shining light from above, no chorus of angels. Gilded with rainbows it wasn't.

But an epiphany it was.

Everything I had previously assumed was suddenly so turned on it's head and so shockingly antithetical to what I had discovered, that I wondered: how could any man have even the slightest clue as to what a women wants from him as a lover, unless it was sledge hammered over his skull, as it seemed to be for me.

I never looked at a woman the same way again. I understood them in ways I had never considered. I stopped arguing. I stopped being angry with them.

I marveled at my own ignorance.

James Cahill

A fifteen-minute debacle.

Jenny and I were at the drugstore looking over a display of contraceptives. In the past she had been on the pill, which, she said, made her depressed and fat. An I.U.D. was out of the question for some medical reason. Foams and sponges left us both burning.

Then she happened upon something we hadn't seen before. We pulled it off the shelf and read the instructions. 1) Administer. 2) Wait fifteen minutes.

Easy enough!

That night, in a stunning bit of gallantry, I managed instruction number one myself.

Then: fifteen minutes.

I checked the clock on the dresser, calculated ahead a quarter lap around the luminescent dial.

I kissed her. I touched her a bit here, some there.

I glanced at the clock. One minute, fifteen seconds had elapsed.

I exhaled and kissed her again. Her mouth, her breasts. I smooched around on her stomach. I caressed her legs, massaged her calves a bit. I stole another glance at the clock. Only three minutes gone.

Had time ever crept so slowly? I rubbed her neck, glanced at the clock. I massaged her shoulders, glanced at the clock.

I hummed a song, tapped the beat on her back. I went over a list of things I had to do tomorrow.

I checked the time. *Just five and a half minutes?*

I was soon on the brink of insanity.

What in hell kind of contraceptive was this? Was it designed by some malignant demon to prevent pregnancy by forcing me to slit my own throat? Fifteen minutes! I was ready to claw my own flesh; rip out chunks of hair and fling them across the room.

Here was the woman I loved, naked and willing. And I couldn't make love to her! I might have been staring at her from a prison cell across the room!

I only wanted relief! Pure, sweet, blessed relief!

But no. I had to contend with these fifteen wretched minutes, only seven of which were in the past, and a full eternity of eight stood before me, mocking me, laughing at me.

Finally, with glacial sluggishness, the entire obnoxious quarter of an hour moved into history, and I let go a cry of sweet rapture the instant that second hand hit the twelve.

When it was over, and we both lay sweating and staring up at the ceiling, I thought about what had just occurred. What sort of dazzling repertoire did I have, that I could barely hold out for seven minutes? Why was I so impatient? I'd never had to actually look at a clock before, and frankly, it was quite an education. I saw a poll once in some magazine where women said they liked between 14 and 25 minutes of foreplay, but rarely got it. What was fifteen minutes? In the calm of post-coital retrospect, I wondered: what the hell was wrong with me?

I remembered a past lover or two who had said: *Wait, I'm not ready-*

Even Jenny, early on, had said the same. But there I was, proceeding whether she was ready or not. Get her wet, I assumed, and the tedious work of foreplay was over. Right? Wasn't this it? Wasn't this annoying, frustratingly consistent female demand satisfied? You did your best, certainly, yet every man I knew, in fact, if we discussed it, complained about his woman's desire for *more foreplay*.

But this was a new relationship. This brevity on my part hadn't become a battleground yet. We were still in that realm of careful politeness, where any comment other than 'everything you do is wonderful' would hit like blasphemy. We were months from brutal honesty. But this woman was special. I saw something good here, and I wanted this relationship. This was the woman I loved, but I couldn't even give her fifteen brief minutes of touching.

I just wanted to enter her. Everything else was truly incidental, in fact, a nuisance.

I thought back again on my love affairs of the past. What, in truth, did I know about sex? You get your woman wet, then enter. But how many times had I heard:

"Not yet!"

"It's too soon!"

"I'm not ready!"

But I proceeded anyway. Why? Because, by God, *I* was ready.

I considered the phrase again: "Go slow...be gentle." These words meant nothing to me. They had struck me as a reprimand, a bad progress report.

And after this overly swift and embarrassing debacle, in which I might have deluded myself into thinking that - like Pierre - I had impetuously taken her beneath the moonlight, my woman was unhappy. Silent and disappointed.

Karen had told me nearly all of her female friends claimed they didn't like sex or were indifferent. How could this be possible? To not like sex! The single activity that virtually informed my every thought and action, tormenting me every waking moment and many sleeping moments too. I certainly did not wish my beautiful, beloved Jenny to be one of these women. But I could see, with some trepidation, that we were headed unavoidably in this direction. Down the road, I saw us with prophetic clarity, making love one miserable night a week - or month - and even then, after a battle, or some coaxing that was finally humiliating.

After my hideous fifteen-minute performance, my disaster of impatience, I thought: What were these things I had dismissed so quickly as a reprimand?

Go Slow. Be Gentle.

The following morning we used the contraceptive again. And I vowed: I would not focus with single-minded mania on the goal of intercourse. I would give her this fifteen minutes as a gift, rather than do battle with it. Well, *somewhat* as a gift. Was I so noble, so magnanimous? A shoe-in for sainthood? Not quite. In this fifteen minutes, I would try out this annoying advice - to go slow and be gentle – to give it a road test, if only to prove that it was complete nonsense. Almost to spite all the women who had ever uttered such a miserable phrase. As if to say, 'See! It's rubbish and now will you quit pestering me and let me love you as I see fit, without all your foolish demands!' And just to underscore my point, by God, I would perform this request with gusto. I would touch her with excruciating slowness. I would be supremely gentle. Only then could I legitimately say, *"Ha! There! You see!"*

So, in this spirit - generous but vengeful - or, as Lady Macbeth said, 'The flower with the serpent beneath't,' I began.

I touched her slowly, gently. I kissed her cheek... her lips... her neck. I took my luscious time. I touched her arm - her forearm, inside, slowly up to where it bends, then down the outside... to her hand, to each... of... her fingers. I moved at blissful leisure. I traced my fingers lightly around her palm. And a peculiar thing happened. Moving so slowly forced me, strangely, to focus on my touch. When I touched her back, I focused *only* on touching her back. I didn't think about why I was touching her back. I wasn't touching her back because this would get me where I wanted to be in a moment. I was simply... touching... her back. I moved my hand, lightly, slowly, over her shoulders, along her spine, over each of shoulder blades. It occurred to me: I'd never really noticed her shoulder blades before. They were small, feminine. With infinite patience, I outlined each of them with my fingertips. I touched her ribs, one at a time, then moved down to her lower back, and lightly graced my fingers over those two dimples above her tush. What are these for, I wondered. I touched that wonderful crease between the top of her thigh and her lovely bottom. I touched her forehead, her eyebrows. Her cheeks. Slowly, gently. Focusing always on my touch.

My first amazement: I was able to do this!

The impatience for intercourse: It's a myth! I had been one of the 'get her wet, get inside, then hammer away for as long as you can hold out' crowd. (Though I hoped a verb slightly better than 'hammer' would apply.) Fifteen minutes was nothing! When I actually did touch her slowly and gently, focusing on my touch, the impatience was gone! *I was able to do this.* Once I dismissed the goal, and focused on the moment by moment of the journey, an entire world opened up that I did not know existed. Had I not had this experience - performed half out of spite - I wouldn't even know about it. I finally understood what women had been telling me, what they seem to have been shouting at men in every language since lovemaking began.

James Cahill

My second amazement: To love this way was foreign to anything I had ever done before. My previous efforts at foreplay were always fraught with panic. I was too rushed, perhaps too excited. My touch had no poise, no sense of it's own isolated dignity, none of the magic I suddenly experienced. When I touched Jenny now, each caress existed in one bubble of time. I noticed it, enjoyed it, and then moved on to the next. Previously, I touched as if going down a list - you had to do this and this and this, get them all over with - before you could do what you wanted. I didn't enjoy each moment so why should she? All was aimed at an event soon to occur - when I could finally, with a sigh of relief, finish this nonsense and engage in what I thought was the real business of lovemaking.

The final amazement: Strangest, most wonderful of all; I had never seen Jenny enjoy my caresses so much! Or any woman for that matter! But beyond focusing on my touch, even more wonderful was focusing on her *reaction* to my touch. She languished like a cat. I could hear changes in her breathing, an occasional gasp, a delightful moan. Even if she said nothing, her silence told me her attention was riveted on the delicate movement of my fingers. *I was pleasing her!* I was making the woman I loved feel wonderful!

And it was easy! Not a tedious burden at all. In fact, this slow, gentle, focused touching was infinitely easier than my haste of the past. And I wondered: why this impetuous rush to enter? Calm down. Focus on the present. Touch her in the timeless now.

Other myths also fell by the wayside. The first was that a vast repertoire of gymnastic techniques and positions, though perhaps fun to experiment with, and useful for one reason or another were far less important than this slow, gentle, focused touching.

The second myth to go by the wayside - and a very polyannish one - was this: love itself would guide your fingers, your lips. I learned that, in fact, men and women possess no instinct for how to best erotically touch a partner of the opposite sex.

J   J   J

Tony excused himself to use the restroom. If the waitress came by I was to order him a second pint of Skank.

I looked around. Our little slip of a waitress - cute enough to make your teeth ache - was nowhere in sight. I had a sudden, passing curiosity as to whether restaurants ever faced discrimination lawsuits. *They wouldn't hire me, your honor, because I wasn't hot enough.*

And my thoughts were sparked and simmering. All this lusty chat was inclining me in a strange direction. I thought: *Maureen.* Our department secretary. I had toyed with the idea whimsically, sitting in my office, grading papers. I had never actually considered such an act in all of its thrilling possibility.

But this evening *was mine.*

Where was I?

Out with Tony, by God. Yakking it up with an old friend. If I returned home two hours late, who would be the wiser? 'Out with Tony' was pure truth, nothing less.

Could I actually pull this off?

Well, I could call. I could suss things out; test the waters. Momo. She hadn't exactly been unfriendly the past few weeks.

The waitress appeared, now busy at another table. I waved and she nodded to me.

Was it such a big deal? Didn't these things happen all the time?

"Nice shirt," Maureen had told me just last week, gliding her lovely fingers over my ribs. Or, "Did you get the notice about the department meeting?" her hand on my forearm.

I meant it when I told Tony I had never had an affair. I hadn't. Not one, though nearly every man I knew had had one. And they talked about them. It made me wonder which was more important - the affair or telling friends about it afterwards.

But then, what did I know of such things?

Who was I kidding, I thought, as the waitress glided toward me, just as Tony returned. We ordered pints and took a long sip when they arrived.

"Nothing like a tall, cold pint of Muskrat Skank," Tony said. "Kinda takes the edge off the day, don't you think?"

I said that it did.

"This slow and gentle touching," he said. "I can't tell you how intrigued I was. And I was only just beginning with this stuff. It gets better."

T   T   T

I tried it again that evening.

I was still staggered by my discovery. I could take time and my Jenny loved it. Go slow, be gentle, was not a reprimand, not an attack on my virility, competence, or, as a friend says with a lusty wink, my cocksmanship. It was no attack at all. Only a mere suggestion. A suggestion that for some reason, until then, I didn't understand. My impatience to culminate the event in intercourse was now easily discarded. And here I was: a man, stark naked, thoroughly aroused, and beside me was my lovely woman, also, naked as a jaybird. In a situation that normally rendered me half insane, I was, instead, for the second time in my life, poised, calm, patient.

I kissed my lovely Jenny. I placed my hand on her back. Just my fingertips. I moved them, from her shoulder blade to the edge of her clavicle, slowly and gentle as a breeze, gracing now her spine, now the small of her back.

In the past - as early as the day before - I never wasted time with a back. Once, a previous girlfriend had even told me she liked her back rubbed. I gave her back a cursory glancing with my fingers, but for the most part, I ignored her request. What a fool I was, but I thought, what was a back? Other places were infinitely more interesting. A back was certainly nothing worth the bother of someone who knew clearly, desperately, what he wanted and how to get there.

But now there was no desperation. None at all.

I touched her back.

Slowly.

I touched her face.

I had all the time in the world.

Patiently, I touched her shoulders.

I noticed them.

What smooth...delightful...skin.

I focused my attention precisely where I touched her. This is Jenny's back. Her smoooooth back. This is how her back feels. Soft. Warm.

A meditative calm fell over me. I listened to her breath. I could even feel her heart beating. She lay there, my Jenny, under my slow, gentle touch, as if in silent, accepting ecstasy. I felt so calm, so unhurried. It was even better than this morning! I had never done this: been naked with a woman, and felt so calm and focused.

To my astonishment once again, Jenny's breath quickened. I had done nothing but touch her back, but her breath had quickened! Her back! A decidedly unerrogenous zone! Certainly, until that miraculous day, one of the less interesting places. But no longer. Jenny was writhing like a cat! And now, a whisper of the old instinct told me: okay, you've gotten her started - now, faster, and harder and you'll soon find yourself entering the blessed Garden of-

But no.

No, no, no.

I moved my hands even more slowly. Slower than I could believe. Slower and lighter than I have ever touched a woman before.

Her breath quickened again.

She moaned.

I had made my woman moan! And would it be too obnoxious, too self-congratulatory to say, *in ecstasy?* Why not? I'll say it! My Jenny moaned in ecstasy! I was nowhere in the vicinity of *any* body part that should elicit such a response. But there it was. A sweet, lovely moan.

I ran my fingers over her stomach - slowly, lightly, gently. As slowly as possible.

We joke about children not coming with instructions. Either do women. Skin itself - all of it - is an erogenous zone. A light, gracing glance of fingertips is an erotic touch.

Who explains this to us?

No one.

Instead we grope like impatient fools. But I was learning.

J   J   J

I excused myself to use the bathroom. But I didn't *just* use the bathroom. (This *but not just* construction. A partial truth? A lie of omission?) Just outside the restroom, I called my wife Cindy to tell her I'd be late. She was silent. I could hear Christopher and Julie in the background watching TV. "What's going on?" she said.

"Chatting with Tone," I said, "like I told you."

She went silent again. Then, "You sure?"

"Cin. My God. Will you stop?" Ever since that little misunderstanding - with none other than Maureen - Cindy seemed unusually inquisitive. "It's been awhile. You know Tony. He has a lot to say."

"Don't be too late," she said.

We said our good-byes. I hung up. I glanced around, took a breath of resolution. I made a second call on the cell phone. One ring... two...

"Hello?"

"Maureen?"

"Jim?"

"Yo, Momo. Busy?"

"Busy watching the news. Where are you?"

"Out with an old friend. I was wondering. Could I, uh, drop by later?"

"Mmm... I'll consider it."

"Then I'll swing by in a while to see what you decide," I said. This, *I'll consider it*. How did she make plain English so enticing? I then dipped an intrepid toe into the raging current. "So, what are you wearing at this very moment?"

Maureen let go a languid exhale. "What do you think I'm wearing?"

"Well, in my mind, Momo, please don't hate me, but I must tell you, quite candidly, *in my mind*, you're stark staring, screaming, raving-"

"Mister Jimster. Naughty Jimster. You have quite an imagination."

"Thank you."

We hung up.

Life. An enigma wrapped in a riddle wrapped in a conundrum. I hadn't actually done a thing with Maureen. All that occurred was a lot of steamy double entendres in the Department office with no one in earshot, and then I headed back to my own office, sat at my desk, and percolated. I tried to prepare a lecture but all I could think of was Maureen, with her bright red lips and her sweet, leisurely voice. I took Maureen out to lunch once. We live in a small town. Cindy heard about it somehow. She questioned me, and I told her it was work related. Which it was. And I thought: *but not just...* Cindy's silence told me she didn't buy it.

My romantic life with Cindy had cooled precipitously since our first year together. It had cooled, and I had been good. I had always been good. But lately, my own thoughts seemed to undermine me. Former vaporous fantasies were suddenly begging for tangible manifestation. I was, in a word, going crazy, and suddenly, there was Maureen. Her lips always seemed... so red, so shiny and wet. Always, an agonizing bit of lace seemed to peek from beneath her blouse. Was a bit of self-indulgence such a crime? Though I'd fantasized about Maureen extensively, even at times, and I hate to admit, during a rare bout of lovemaking with Cindy, I had not touched her. And if I did touch her - a woman other than my wife - well, to which level of hell would I be consigned?

If Cindy didn't find out, what difference would it make? I had no idea. Milan Kundera's surgeon in The Unbearable Lightness of Being, had countless affairs and said, "This has nothing to do with my wife." It drove his wife insane with jealousy, but I understood him. I agreed: nothing to do with his wife! I had literary support. Would any woman understand? Unlikely.

What is it about certain women; they seem to ignite the most basic, primordial embers in you? And then, with the fire raging, you had to make a decision.

A decision, certainly, but between what and what? A brief bit of self-indulgent sinning? Or saintly denial? Heaven or Hell? Truth be told, which was which? To deny myself such an opportunity felt like pure hell. To fall into Maureen's lovely arms... well, I couldn't imagine a better paradise. It was true, as I told Tony, I had never had an affair, but this could end in a few short hours.

Who would know?

What would it cost?

Even now, I trembled with pure anticipation as if the thing was happening already; as if it was out of control and I was careening headlong down a dark, enchanting path.

We ordered cheeseburgers. They made excellent hamburgers: char-broiled half-pounders, with aged cheddar cheese, bacon if you wanted, and a near-endless pile of French fries.

"I used to meditate," Tony said. "I once attended a week-long Zen meditation retreat in a beautiful, wooded setting in the mountains. The leader, a Caucasian man in his mid-fifties approached the podium while we sprawled on our zafus over the carpeted floor of a large hall. He moved to the microphone with patient, deliberate steps. He looked over his group with supreme attention and serenity. He spoke slowly, choosing his words with care.

"'In meditation,' Tony said, imitating the teacher's saintly, mystical voice, "'we breathe mindfully. We listen to our heartbeat mindfully. In life, this is also the case. When we walk, we step mindfully. When we observe the world, we look with our fullest consciousness. When we listen, we hear with complete attention. We eat mindfully. We focus upon each bite. Taste it, experience it. We live with our fullest awareness each moment.'"

"The man finished his speech and moved slowly, patiently, with the attentiveness his philosophy demanded, back to his chair. Later that day, I wandered into the kitchen. There was the Zen master, as if exhausted from so much mindfulness, wolfing down glazed, jelly doughnuts and reading a magazine." Tony shook his head, took a bite of his burger, which dripped with ketchup. After a moment, he said, "But who's to say, if the man practiced what he preached - in the bedroom at least, if not the kitchen - he probably made his woman very happy."

After a few thoughtful bites, Tony continued.

T   T   T

My titanic struggle with fifteen minutes, and the change that occurred, was for me, the dawning of a new era. But just a dawning. I had spoken with men, with women, and with Colleen the Anthropologist. I had experienced this strange event that occurred partly out of spite, but that gave me a glimpse into a new world. It was just a glimpse and I still had yet to step through the door completely. But the glimpse was two-sided. I saw that an entire world I hadn't known awaited me, but a glance over my shoulder from this new vantage point gave me an inkling of what all these women were talking about. And I wondered: How universal was the problem? Though everyone I spoke with suggested it was, how big was my sample? Was it a big, big problem, as Colleen had insisted?

A couple I knew, Richard and Joanna, were discussing a friend - a woman named Sharon - who was about to get married. Sharon had announced: "When I'm married, my husband can have me anytime he wants."

Richard saw no problem with this, but Joanna was incensed. "Can you believe a woman would say such a thing? Anytime he wants!"

They asked what I thought.

The 'anytime' part was fine with me. It was the 'have me' that was troubling. Why should he have her at all? Such a phrase implies that he will use her and give her nothing. If this was the agreement, then Joanna was rightfully annoyed. Was her declaration some antediluvian expression of gratitude to her husband for marrying her, and thus, being available for his sexual and other needs? Is it only *she* who gives *him* pleasure?

If we can't hide in bedrooms and evaluate the erotic give and take between men and women, perhaps our language more readily reveals us. If a man 'has her', or 'gets some' or 'takes her', it seems fair to say that the man makes demands, and that the woman either gives in or sets limits. Sex, for a man, seemed a matter of whether she'd let you, not whether she wanted to.

Was this the scenario of every couple?

What did I - or anyone - really know of sex?

In ninth grade, our friend Kam explained something to me called the 'base system'. It was a junior high method of understanding the hierarchical progression of sex. First base was a kiss. Second was touching a girl's breasts. Third was touching her down below - graphically called 'finger banging', euphemistically called 'heavy petting'. A home run was intercourse. Interestingly, it was also a precise barometer to measure the prowess of a boy, and, conversely, the looseness of a girl. If a boy got second, by God, we wanted to know who the slut was who gave it to him. And once we knew, everyone knew. But the girl was not exactly a slut, in that she didn't only receive the derision we usually heap upon the morally downfallen. I remember a girl named Francesca, who went to second base with a guy named Keith.

Francesca. A tramp, certainly, but she was now, also, the bearer of sweet, dark mysteries, the erotic heroine of my secret, adolescent fantasies. I watched her with solemn wonder as she the performed the pedestrian tasks of going to her locker, of eating her lunch.

"Look at her!" Kam said, "Just *eating her lunch!*"

Oh, the magic of Francesca!

But this base system. To hit a home run was to have truly made it. The boy who hits a home run develops a knowing way about him. He struts. He gives advice. We listen.

But why does a man *have* a woman? Why does a woman *give it up*, another phrase that seems to betray our attitude? I remember endless discussions regarding which girls '*gave*' and which didn't. Why was it always women doing the giving?

The problem is this: we make it around the base pads, and then we stop. Not much changes since ninth grade, in our language or our behavior. This is it, we assume. The homerun. This is the end of the line, all there is.

Well, it isn't.

How does the typical male define a good lover? Men approach the subject from a vast and safe distance. The chitchat and jokes suggest that a man's notion of a good lover might be this: a huge, everlasting hard-on. In junior high, high school, even in college and beyond, 'Little dick' jokes and premature ejaculation jokes were quite popular.

"Craig jacks off with tweezers!"

AH HA HA HA HA HA!

"Fred's done in five seconds!"

AH HA HA HA HA HA!

We've heard it. We've been victims of it.

So what made a man a good lover? I asked a few women what usually takes place prior to intercourse. Their answers were disturbingly consistent. "When men want sex, the extent of their flirtation is to say, 'You got a great ass.' Then, with a minimum of foreplay – he kisses her lips, touches her breasts, touches her down below, and - sex begins." He enters her well before she's ready, hammers away, etc., then rolls over and goes to sleep. Many women, it appeared, went through life, tragically, knowing no pleasure in sex at all.

Female Euphemism

The language of men is graphic.

We aren't under the moral gun to behave and speak with an eye for a wholesome, noble presentation to the world. Our language is edgier, earthier, certainly less vague. A woman may say, "Tom was caring, sensitive," but the nuts and bolts of Tom's sensitivity are a mystery. Somehow, this is enough information for the female ear. I would wonder: What exactly does Tom do that makes him romantic? But Tom, if he's my good friend, will tell me exactly how Sheila kissed him and where. He will name the places, describe precisely what she did with her hands, her legs, etc. He may lower his voice. He certainly will if a woman is in earshot. Chances are, this hypothetical woman in earshot will be disgusted - or at least, highly judgmental of the revelation of such detail. But we're men, and our language matches our thought process. We think and fantasize in shockingly graphic detail. (However, I have met a few women who are wonderfully graphic and open.)

Women, I'm told, have more emotional fantasies. The booming market for romance novels underscores this difference. Such books typically lack graphic sex. They appeal to the powerful emotional aspect of female psychology and sell like gangbusters. The latest feminine craze for vampire books and movies is also about intense desire that is not consummated. Women spend fortunes on such entertainment. Female language, too, is more grounded in emotion. And emotional language, though loftier in tone, is vague. Take time. Go slow. Be gentle. Show you care. Woo me. Be romantic. Show some affection.

As a man, I hear this, and I think, fine, okay, now please tell me what to do with my hands. Such language leaves us clueless. And another, inadvertent interpretation - though quite subtle - is that the woman's desires are loftier than his. Hers are on a higher moral plane, while his are more at the level of the gutter. As men, this tweaks us, shoves a little dagger into us, with the painful implication that we're cretinous vulgarians. It implies that our efforts in bed fall short because we're drooling, unsophisticated swamp creatures.

So the language tells us nothing, and – inadvertently or not – it insults us. When we're reeling from such an attack - imagined or real - it's difficult to hear anything. I say imagined or real. I don't believe women intend to hurt us with such language. Moral loftiness is simply important to many women, and they would like us to notice this aspect of them, appreciate it, and to express it in how we treat them in and out of bed. Most of us miss this entirely. We feel hurt, and are unable to take in the real message. The advice a woman gives a man, results at best, in kind of grudging foreplay; a touching men do to placate women, but that we - and they - don't really enjoy.

But euphemistic language is only the beginning of the problem.

It gets worse.

Male Competence

Why are there three million sperm and only one egg? Because men hate to ask directions.

A competent man knows what he's doing. A suggestion offered by a woman implies that we don't, and our competence - and our very manhood - falls into question. Thus, we prefer to get hopelessly lost rather than reveal our incompetence by asking directions. Sadly, many of us are also hopelessly lost in the bedroom. Even the slightest suggestion, phrased politely or not, can cause us to feel attacked, rendering us unable to listen, and certainly unable to change.

A woman says: "Go slow, be gentle."

A man hears: "You're incompetent, vulgar, and unmanly."

Nothing changes. An argument is often the result.

When I had a glimmer of what women mean when they say, 'go slow, be gentle,' I tried to explain it to my friend Tom, who had confided that lovemaking with his wife had fallen off to once a month and he was going crazy.

I didn't tell him that Jenny and I were at it daily, often twice. I only said to him, "Do you take time with her?"

"*Shit!*" he said. "I hear that crap from my wife all the time! I don't *have* time!"

I had a similar conversation with several other men, and I realized that I needed a better way to explain this. I couldn't simply use the language of women. It is not a language men understand. And it's inadvertently threatening.

Sexual competence, one of many types of competence that men simply believe they should possess, as if by instinct, is a subject fraught with insecurity. Among those who prey on this insecurity are surgeons who collect small fortunes to perform penile lengthening operations. Ironically, a man with such an operation, in the throes of passion, is no bigger, and he basically just hangs a bit longer for the men in the locker room at the gym.

It's an odd but telling story of how misdirected our motives are. Rather than actually learning to please our women, we are content to have other men believe we are good at pleasing them. This focus on the perception of competence - rather than *actual* competence - be it from other men or, or simply within ourselves, is nothing less than fascinating. In fact, the entire male enhancement industry – in all of its incarnations - gives men the wrong message.

Why Colleen said, "But you have to!"

All women could relate to the Meg Ryan fake orgasm scene? How is this possible?

Sharon is unhappy with the way her husband Jonathan makes love to her. She offers a suggestion; her husband is hurt. His competence, his manliness is under assault. He doesn't understand her wholesome, euphemistic language. Go slow, take time, be gentle – these words hit him like the language of a saint, pronouncing him, not only inept, but also vulgar. He grows silent. Perhaps an argument ensues. He may sulk for days.

She thinks: Well, that didn't work. Consciously or unconsciously, she knows her suggestion failed, and now, something worse is amiss in the relationship.

The orgasm! The barometer of our virility! If a woman critiques our lovemaking, we sulk. If she lays in silence without any sort of detonation, we sulk. We're incompetent, unmanly. But our women love us, hate to see us unhappy, or simply can't stand to put up with us in such a state.

So she fakes one. What would it hurt? And if we think about it, what choice does she have? We don't listen to her advice because it's either too painful or two vague. She would like us to do better, but any attempt she makes to improve things makes us miserable, even angry.

Do we really want them to protect us like this? Are we so delicate?

I'm told of another scenario, which is even more distressing. Nothing the man does as he makes love to his woman is pleasing her. Statistics show that women climax less than 30% of the time through intercourse alone. In the 70% (or more) of the time that she does not come, she doesn't simply shrug her shoulders and say, "Oh well, better luck next time." She isn't properly warmed up, and often, she isn't even wet. While he's blithely pumping away, he may even be hurting her. Nothing he's doing feels good to her, and it could very well be painful. She knows she can't say, "Please, just stop," without crushing his ego and risking an argument. So, just to end it without rancor, she fakes an orgasm.

Mary, a previous girlfriend, told me I was rushing, not thinking of her. I got angry. I stormed out. And I felt smug in the truly unbelievable notion that, by God, I had drawn the line. *This is what I would take. This is what I wouldn't take. Mess with me and see where it gets you.*

If we all behave like this - I can see why a woman might fake an orgasm. And I can see why all women could relate to the Meg Ryan scene. Even if women don't perform this blissed-out sham every time, even if they just do it once in awhile, what sort of comment is this on our sex lives as a whole? It means women don't feel free to give us any suggestions. It's simply too dangerous. In means they can tell us nothing at all unless it's a compliment. If it's a lie, like a fake orgasm, we're placated but we remain inept.

And this, much worse realization: not only are we not pleasing them, but we're actually *hurting them*. I conducted an informal poll. I knew several women who had many lovers, some upwards of a hundred. I asked them what percentage of men knew how to touch a woman intimately. Their answers were alarming but consistent. "About ten, twenty percent." So about eighty-five percent of us – that's nearly everyone, and in the past I had certainly been among them - don't know what we're doing when it comes to the very important business of touching and pleasing a woman. I would guess that percentage is higher among young people.

If every woman could relate to Meg Ryan's fake orgasm scene, it also means this: typical sex has no other purpose than to relieve a

James Cahill

man's physical need and feed his ego. And women get little or nothing out of lovemaking. And if sex does become painful, this certainly explains why a woman will often rebuff her man's future attempts
to make love.

Thank you, Meg, for that eye-opener of a scene.

And though most women are tactful in making suggestions,
sometimes, due to a misguided sense of feminism, they can be downright mean. Once, in my early twenties, my inexperience and zeal got
the best of me. I was with a new partner for the first time and things
happened a bit too quickly. She exhaled and said, "Already?"

"Sorry."

Then she said, "Oh, just do something with your hand."

I did.

I did something with my hand, but I had no idea what she
wanted me to do. She wouldn't tell me and I was already too hurt
and too miserable to ask. Finally, she pushed my hand away, and
with a lung full of disgust told me, "You're so macho! So selfish!"

Macho? Selfish? I had no idea what she was talking about.

I rolled over - silent, crushed, devastated.

How I survived, recovered, and climbed back on the horse is a
story of courage that would bring tears to your eyes.

I never saw this woman again. We parted angrily, and in ter-
rific misunderstanding. She was as ignorant as I, though she was
equipped with some feisty, misplaced feminist rhetoric.

Later, I learned to fight back when met with such an attack.

Later still - after the sea change - I discovered I didn't have to
fight at all. And I learned this: when a woman makes a suggestion,
a good lover listens without feeling attacked, hurt, or defensive. A
good lover simply hears a suggestion and makes adjustments. All
lovers should say aloud to each other: I will not take your suggestions as attacks, or as expressions of my incompetence. They are, in
fact, opportunities for me to improve my ability to please you. To
make me a better lover. More competent. Whatever I want to tell
you; whatever you want to tell me: it is safe for either of us to say

anything. Nothing is to be taken personally. Again, this oath should be spoken aloud, and it should be revisited frequently.

How can I possibly know what another person feels or needs - particularly a person with a different brain and different set of parts than I have, when no one sat me down and explained it. And certainly, when most of my information from other men arrives in the form of put-downs or self-promotion.

When people discuss sex, everyone agrees: communication is important. But communication is another vague term with a saintly glow, and everyone nods sagely at its utterance, then goes home and nothing changes. The problem involves much more than simple communication. This is a very sensitive area. Couples must agree to an atmosphere of safety. Suggestions should be made gently and kindly. They should be heard with openness, acceptance, gratitude, and a sense of opportunity. And consider: A good lover is not always the person who knows what to do, but the person who is comfortable with the state of *not knowing*, able to listen, ready to learn.

Do something with your hand, she said to me.

I will soon describe exactly what it is a man can do with his hand that will give his woman pleasure she has never known. But such things are far from obvious. A female body, and the woman herself, is a mystery; the vagina, an infinite confusion of fluids and flesh.

To a man, 'Do something with your hand,' is yet another impossibly vague request. A man has no vagina, so he has no idea what this something might be. A premature ejaculation is not an act of selfishness or the result of a macho persona. It's normal, and depending on a woman's level of empathy, it can be very embarrassing.

We get ridicule from men and often, criticism from women. We take innocent suggestions as criticism. We get soft-soaped by caring - or frustrated - women who fake orgasms. Is it any wonder men have difficulty knowing what a woman wants?

And if male insecurity, fake orgasms, feminine vagueness, and a female body that is a complete mystery don't create enough problems, well, it becomes even more difficult.

J   J   J

Our lovely waitress returned to inquire if we needed anything.
We both looked at her for a moment.
She smiled, and we said that we didn't.
When she was gone, Tony said, "Want to hear a strange story?"
"All ears," I said.

T   T   T

Seduce me
My friend Jason dated two different women within a few months of each other. With each woman, he ended up in bed. Both events had a decidedly casual, consensual feel. All coaxing toward the bedroom seemed fabulously mutual. He did not call either woman afterwards. He felt no impulse to call, saw no reason why he should call. Frankly, he didn't give it much thought either way. Both were bright women and in good graduate schools. He'd had a nice time and hoped they did too. And Jason was buried in his own graduate work.

A time elapsed before he spoke with each of the women over the phone regarding some other, insignificant topic. Oddly, both women, in separate conversations, brought up the date they'd had, and both referred to it, not as the time they slept together, but instead, as the time that Jason had seduced them.

Both women used precisely the same language: The time *you seduced me*.

Jason swore to me, he did not burn a single kilocalorie towards seducing either of them. He wasn't bragging. He wouldn't have told me about it otherwise, if not for this very odd coincidence. Both women, in fact, found their way into his bed in an act of stunning, shared decision making that would make any feminist proud. In the case of one, he felt, in fact, that she did *more* of the coaxing toward the bedroom.

None of this tale was aimed at his own self-aggrandizement. He was just mystified by the situation.

To put it simply, why did two bright, strong women, tell a man he seduced them when, in his opinion, both made a clear choice to go to bed with him.

To understand this, we need to try to think the way women think.

This is not easy to do, but necessary.

A psychiatrist once told me that, in trying to understand people, the mistake most people make is that they expect others to think the way they, themselves think. We are shocked, he said, when we discover that other people think differently. Further, he believes, as a therapist, he can only begin to help a patient when he can tune in to their thoughts so well that he can actually begin to predict with accuracy what they are about to say.

In the same way, we need to understand how women think in order to know how to please them. To cross the abyss between the differing thought patterns of women and men is to make a leap of courage, generosity, and empathy, and to find a fascinating world of infinite strangeness on the other side. This other world has a different color and texture for each person, but once there, we'll discover consistencies among nearly all women, and much that has baffled us will begin to make sense.

(We'll return to the women Jason didn't seduce in a moment.)

In a similar vein - that of leaping across the abyss - another friend, Steven, once, out of the blue, told me he thought he could imagine what it was like to have a vagina. An intriguing notion! I tried it myself. I cleared my thoughts: A vagina. Okay. An odd flatness. An opening. A curious feeling of wetness now and again. At this point, I gave up. Though I admired the courageousness of Steven's efforts, I doubted his success. There must be an infinite amount to know about having a vagina that extends far beyond simple physical parameters.

James Cahill

I was fascinated by the question. I had failed in the effort to understand physically what it's like. But I wondered if I could understand the *experience* of having a vagina. For days, I thought about this.

A Precious Gift

Of course, I take a risk here. Someone who actually *has* a vagina might quickly tell me, give it up. Stick with what you know. I only ask: indulge me. Humor me. This is truly a crude effort. A leap that may, finally, be very embarrassing. But bear in mind; the goal is to help men understand women in order to learn to please them. A woman can't explain it to a man. What would she say? *"It's like, well, a vagina, dummy!"* And we'd remain oblivious.

How is a man to understand a woman without beginning here? At best, he can make rough, ballpark guesses. If he approaches any kind of accuracy, well, everyone gains. So, with complete trepidation, I shall proceed. I only ask; if you actually have one, go easy on me.

To be a woman, to have a vagina, and to make love, I believe, feels something like this:

As children, we played a game called 'Trust'. One child, with eyes closed, stands in the center of a circle of friends. The child leans this way, and that way, while his friends catch and push him back to the center.

A woman making love is like the child in the middle. When she offers herself to a man, she leans in his direction with her eyes closed, and in this leaning, add the idea that she not only gives a man great pleasure, but, in her mind, she feels herself bestowing upon him an incredible gift. In fact, her most precious gift. But of course, in leaning, she places herself in danger, which is why the game is called trust.

For the man to proceed with intercourse before she's ready, or, to please himself and let her languish while he gets himself a beer and flips on a ball game or just goes to sleep, is tantamount to stepping aside and letting her fall onto the hard concrete. She feels used,

48

hurt, and dirty; what are the odds that she'll want to play this game with him again?

Chances are, she won't.

But... Jason. Jason who didn't seduce the two women. I don't know whether Jason is a good or bad lover. But he didn't call the women afterwards. They leaned and he let them fall to the concrete.

Imagine you're a woman. You crave love, at certain times of the month, as much as any man. You give a man your most precious gift. You wait for his response. He does nothing to show that he cares for you or appreciates the gift you have given him.

You feel used, as if you'd been dragged through a cesspool.

How does a woman reconcile such an event in her mind without feeling like some vile swamp creature? The feminine solution to this problem is a marvel of mental gymnastics.

Good Girl/Bad Girl - Strange Middle Ground

Whereas a man can be cavalier about sex, a woman doesn't give herself up lightly. For a woman to be sexually active, she must first reconcile herself with the good girl/bad girl dichotomy. Women - and men - divide the female sex into two, harshly distinct categories. The Good Girl, who avoids sex - certainly outside of marriage - and The Bad Girl who indulges in sex. But all women need to be touched and loved. How can a woman make love to a man without feeling used, and without feeling like a bad girl?

One option, of course, is that she can choose never to have sex again. Certainly, with this choice, she will never feel bad again. But the desire for sex is strong and real. She needs sex like air and water, but she can't always depend on a man to appreciate her, and to make her feel special afterwards. He may let her down. He may get up; grab a beer and the sports page. He may not call afterwards. He may never call again.

When a man does not show care and appreciation, how does a woman have sex without feeling bad?

Like this: In her mind, she makes it *not her fault*.

How is this accomplished?

She might refer to the event the way Jason's two dates referred to it: *The time he seduced me*, whether he seduced her or not.

You seduced me enables a woman to avoid the bad girl label. If a woman can make the event *not her fault*, but instead, *his*, she can still emerge from the bedroom with her virtue - and good feelings - intact. Thus, it is the *choice* to have sex that truly defines the bad girl. To *end up* having sex through no conscious choice, is vastly higher on a moral continuum. *You seduced me* absolves a woman of responsibility. The man either coerced her or charmed her into bed, but the point is, it's *not her fault*. Other phrases include: *We were swept away! Before we knew it, there we were! One thing lead to another! Fate took its course!* A more current version might be, *I followed my heart*.

It's difficult for men to understand this behavior in women. (Jason certainly didn't.) But we need to try. As the psychiatrist does, and as men, we need to let our minds range beyond our experience and gender and imagine what it's like to be a woman. We need to consider how a woman struggles with the guilt of the bad girl label. How she entrusts a man with her most precious gift - or, metaphorically, as in the game of trust, how she leans in his direction and risks falling to the pavement. And we need to help her, as lovingly as possible, to overcome such feelings.

How do we help her?

Seduce her simply so she can say she was seduced?

Of course, the word seduce has an ugly connotation. It implies, to use, to make someone do something they don't want to do. In truth, no one is ever seduced. We all choose. How we wish to look at an event in retrospect is another story. Let's avoid the word 'seduce'.

Rather, woo her.

She's already decided whether or not she'll make love with you. And she may be waiting for you to accomplish that perfect bit of wooing that will liberate her from guilt.

She needs to see reality - or distort reality - in such a way that the whole event of making love to you is not her fault. This is not mean-spirited or selfish. You will not use her. You will not force her. So, how does a man woo a woman? One way is to take time with her.

Touch her slowly, gently. Give her a good, long, patient warm-up. Let her get lost in your caresses. And she will get lost. She will have a sense of losing control. With your magic touch, you will stoke her passions, as she will see it, beyond her ability to be rational, beyond even her own volition.

Thus, when it's over, she can still feel like a good girl. (Of course, talking to her is another very big aspect of wooing, which we're coming to.)

Seduce her, so that she doesn't suffer any guilt.

Seduction not only gets a woman hot, but also gives her *an excuse.*

If she needs to feel swept away, sweep her away with all of your seductive powers and she will love every bit of it. Seduce her, so she can tell her best friend the next day, "Before I knew it, there I was, in his bed, in his arms." She may even *accuse you* of seducing her, even if, to your memory, you did not burn a single kilocalorie toward her seduction. Feminine guilt connected to sex may be another conundrum men have a difficult time understanding, but men need try to feel empathy and compassion for this lopsided and unfair judgment undergone by women.

Consider how we are taught that sex is sinful, and how this, in turn, causes guilt and a need to blame a partner for responsibility. Though I am not a religious person, I feel compelled to add: When I touch a woman slowly and gently, and use some of the other methods described (later) here to please her, I feel closer to the divine and miraculous than I have ever felt. Patient, graceful, empathetic lovemaking is truly a spiritual experience – uplifting and magical. I hope for a day when sex is no longer considered a sin, and pleasing a partner is recognized as the sacred business that it truly is.

Seduction, wooing, all of this, of course, does not mean men have license to force a women or overwhelm her with persistence. That a woman loves a persistent man - that persistence implies power and virility - is another myth that ought to be dispensed with. If she says no, then it's no. Preliminary touching will soon clarify this.

James Cahill

Touch her hand. Gently touch her thigh. If she pushes your hand away, or holds it down to keep it from moving any further, accept this as her silent answer. Don't be angry. Don't be persistent.

Touch her, because often, any discussion is virtually impossible. To discuss lovemaking beforehand is to make it premeditated, and if it's premeditated, how can she claim afterwards to have been swept away?

All of this can be quite confusing. Once, after a date with a woman named Ann, and after a good hour of kissing and fooling around on her bed, when I felt it was appropriate, I reached for the button of her blouse. She said, no, we should stop, and that I should leave. I politely said that I understood, that I had a wonderful time. And I left. I called her the next day. She said, "I can't believe you left!" I realized then, that her 'no' was an effort to establish a good-girl display of resistance before finally giving in, so as not to appear to be a bad girl – or 'easy' - in her eyes or in mine. In J.D. Salinger's novel, Catcher in the Rye, Holden Caulfield shares his confusion:

"The thing is, most of the time when you're coming pretty close to doing it with a girl, she keeps telling you to stop. The trouble with me is, I stop. Most guys don't. I can't help it. You never really know whether they want you to stop or whether they're just scared as hell, or whether they're just telling you to stop so that if you do go through with it, the blame'll be on you, not them. Anyway, I keep stopping. The trouble is, I get to feeling sorry for them."

While I love Holden's phrase, "blame'll", even more, I admire his compassion. He feels sorry for women because the moral hammer that hovers over them is so powerful, harsh, and unfair. I've been told by some women, no means *wait*, that it's too soon in the relationship for her to make love. But it's crucial for men to remember, 'no' often does mean 'no', and a man should *always* err on the side of caution. If a woman says no, take it, like Holden, as bright red stop sign. If there is confusion, let it be hers. 'No' means 'no'.

When I had a clue about all of this, I paid a visit to Mary. We had made up, and I wanted to discuss it all with her. She smiled, reached to her bookshelf and handed me a book called, *Swept Away*, by Dr. Carol Cassell. I hadn't actually used that phrase yet to describe it, but here it was, a fascinating, thoughtful book, dedicated to the female solution to bad-girl guilt connected to sex.

The precious gift business; the consequent need to be swept away; it isn't to suggest that women only give themselves to a man rarely and grudgingly. Some women might use this method to allow themselves to be sexual with hundreds of men. But, of course, they may not feel free to admit this. I once asked a woman in her late thirties who I knew fairly well how many men she had slept with. Five, she told me. I thought for a moment. This woman loved sex and I couldn't believe she'd been intimate with only five men. I thought for a moment, then asked her if this included one-nighters. She said it didn't, "Because that's not really *sleeping* with someone." The strategies for avoidance of the bad girl label are always fascinating. (And sometimes downright cute.) However, a small percentage of women seem to desire sex and seek it out often and as shamelessly any man. They won't accuse anyone of seducing them. While such women are a delight to encounter and may be quite at home doing the seducing, they will probably still love a slow and gentle warm up.

Most often though - despite the wonderful exceptions - if a woman wants you, she wants you to woo her. (I speak, generally, of Americans. Women in other cultures can behave quite differently in this regard.) Of course, she'll tell you none of this - she may not even be aware of it herself, but know this: it's very difficult to be a woman.

And it is equally difficult to be a man.

J   J   J

We raised our glasses:
To the enigma of women!

To the difficulty of being a man!

"It's difficult to be a man," I said. "I'm feeling a bit sad for myself."

"As you should," Tony said.

"You know," I said, "I was sure you would say, 'but women have it worse.'"

"I'm not sure who has it worse."

"Why?"

Tony took a breath. "That's a tough one."

T   T   T

Why it's Difficult to be a Man.

Think back on your first sexual forays. To kiss a girl. To unbutton a blouse. She won't unbutton it for you. I mean, God bless the woman who will - and as we said, they do exist - but most won't. Why? Because then she's choosing sex in a way that makes her culpable and therefore, easy.

With a new partner, you can sit and joke and hold hands and make double-entendres all night. But finally, you must face a moment of truth. You have to unbutton that blouse. You have to take her hand and walk her to the bedroom. And it can be terrifying. All she has to do is say, "What do you think you're doing?" and you're crushed.

If you don't attempt it, nothing will happen. How many times have I heard a woman say, "He was afraid to try anything," and shake her head in dismay. Or laugh, dismissively. But because she's under a moral hammer, she doesn't want to bear any responsibility.

So you, as the man, *must own the sin so she doesn't have to.* You must be bad, so she can be good in counterpoint. And it's not easy to be bad.

The Appeal of Bad Boys

In every high school, there is always a beautiful, straight-A, church-going girl who is a class officer, president of a club, perhaps a cheerleader, perhaps a star on an athletic team. And she becomes girlfriend of the biggest renegade on campus. He walks with the coolest arrogant strut his low-slung jeans will allow. Legends abound of how he mouths off to teachers, gets drunk on weekends. He once got arrested. His hair falls in his eyes.

People ask: what is *she* doing with *him*?

Some might ask, why do the best women end up with jerks? (Some may suggest that she wants to save him. This rationale appears reasonable, since she is already a saint.)

And: How did he win the girl many see as the best catch on campus?

Consider this best catch. She's the perfect girl. The impulse toward wholesome, parent, teacher, and perhaps even God pleasing behavior is strong in her. But so is a desire to be touched romantically, which is a powerful desire in everyone. In such a young lady's moral universe, the desire to touch and be touched sexually is very bad. The sin is probably heavier for her than for most girls. What is her solution to this problem?

Unconsciously, she seeks out the boy who she knows is unafraid to cross the moral line from good to evil. He seems at home in the world of bad behavior. A boy who is unafraid of sin will be quite willing to *own the sin* of lovemaking so she doesn't have to. His badness will play counterpoint to her goodness. She can be touched and still be wholesome. It's entirely his fault; no one blames her - she does not even blame herself - and he is quite happy to take responsibility.

The Rest of Us.

But for most of us, it's not easy to be bad. Our fathers brought home the money - if we're lucky - but our mothers raised us. We learned about women from a woman's point of view. We're careful around them; some of us are afraid of them. A man must unbutton a blouse, and this act requires tremendous courage. Our mothers don't encourage us to unbutton blouses. They tell us just the opposite, as they should. Sex is for marriage. Respect women. We shouldn't explore forbidden territory. Well, we must. The libido rages long before marriage, and the women around us are torturously tantalizing. Some want us to love them. We must be bad, and if a woman wants to be romantic with us, she wants us to be bad.

Often, she loves it. If she's tiny enough, and we're strong enough, how delighted she is if we lift her up and carry her into the bedroom! By God, it's certainly not her fault then! She didn't even walk to the bedroom! She was literally swept away.

Some women may not want to be carried because they're afraid we'll think she weighs too much. Then, take her by the hand. She may grin and pretend to stumble helplessly.

Of course, we have to be bad, but respectfully bad. Again, no means no. This goes without saying. But this makes the risk of being bad such a delicate, dangerous tightrope walk.

It's difficult for most of us to take this risk, certainly when we're young. A good woman has a wonderful way of saying no. "I'm flattered, but it's just not something I want to do right now." God bless a woman like this. For another, less sensitive woman, the manner in which she says no can be devastating, and at such a moment, you're fair game.

"Is *that* all you want from me?"

"You think I'm just a one-nighter?"

"What exactly do you think you're doing?"

"Is *this* why you asked me out?"

So, for a man too, the path to the bedroom becomes treacherous. Today there's the added aspect of the harassment accusation, which throws the whole nightmare into public and legal judgment. What a man faces: She might make love to him. She might politely say no. She might humiliate him with stinging accusation. She might use the event as an opportunity to strut her virtue by bragging about his failure with her to everyone she knows. She might tell everyone he's a creep. At worst, she might make a formal accusation. If she makes a formal accusation, the question of whether he truly crossed the line or was respectfully wooing must be sorted out.

So, yes, it's hard to be a woman, but it's equally hard to be a man.

A Better Solution

Imagine an anthropologist, heading off into the jungle with pith helmet and note pad, to study a tribe far off in the bush. He or she must suspend cultural prejudice - an ethnocentric worldview - in order to embrace and understand a worldview that is foreign. We must do the same with the person in bed next to us. Here we must suspend our *gender-centric* view, in order to understand the opposite sex. Consider Harry's (Billy Crystal) contention (When Harry Met Sally) that a man can't be friends with a woman because he wants to have sex with every woman he meets. I've heard plenty of men say this, but they would never say it in front of a woman. Consider Meg Ryan's shock at this revelation. Mostly, the female psyche finds the idea of cavalier bed-hopping repugnant. But can a woman suspend her gender-centric bias in order to understand half the people on the planet? Can a man understand that a woman gives up a precious gift when she makes love, and because lovemaking is very emotional for her, she needs to be wooed, and afterwards, she needs to be held and appreciated?

We expect other people to think like us, and they don't.

We must all stretch our thinking, because, here again, male instinct fails us. If a man only looks to his own instincts, he won't get it. When a man makes love to a woman, often, he feels nothing more than as if he's had breakfast with someone. And he feels relief from a lust that has driven him to the brink of insanity.

A woman, on the other hand, feels as though she's given a man her heart and her soul, and that an emotional connection has been forged.

Why should Jason call these women, if, in his mind, the event was tantamount to breakfast? From the ladies point of view, they gave him something very special - and a consequent bond was created - so of course he should call them.

This is the big misunderstanding.

This is why it's so difficult for a man to understand what it's like to have a vagina.

The movie Fatal Attraction played in a fascinating, although grotesque way with these reciprocal misconceptions. Michael

Douglas' character thought he was just having a fling, while Glenn Close's character behaved as if an indelible bond had been created and violated. When I left the theater with my girlfriend, I told her how crazy the woman seemed. Janet listened in silence. Then I added, "I mean, he has sex with her *once*, and she says, 'Live up to your responsibilities!' Please. Give me a-"

Janet stopped dead in her tracks. She looked at me, appalled, and said, "Of *course* he's responsible for her!"

I heard that many similar arguments occurred after that movie.

The Glenn Close character *was* off the deep end, but the importance she placed on sex and the meaning it had for her is fundamental to the majority of women. Whereas most women who are dismissed after a sexual encounter won't boil your pet rabbit, they will almost always feel hurt.

Fatal Attraction creates one extreme, a woman who makes too much of a sexual encounter. Thelma and Louise creates the opposite extreme, men who make too little of one. In this movie, it seems the world is populated with men who see women only as sex objects, and see nothing wrong with using women and shouting lewd comments at them from passing cars. Both excellent movies represent extremes that do exist, but it's wrong to hold either movie up as a final, general statement about members of either sex.

I wondered if all women felt such a connection to a man after sex, as did the Glenn Close character. My friend Karen told me told that yes, all women feel a bond has been created, *and* that the man now cares for her.

This astounded me. A man and a women share an intimacy. Each experiences it so differently. *And each believes the other experiences it the way they themselves do.*

A mess, certainly, but what does it all mean? What do we do with such information? Well, as men, the first thing we must do is this: before we talk blithely about scoring, getting a piece of ass, getting laid, getting some pussy, some action, some tail, some snatch, some poontang, some nookie, or just getting *some*, we should take a breath.

Breathe in, breathe out.

Are we prepared to deliver on the contract that seems crystal clear to nearly all women? The contract that says we are now intimately connected? That we are responsible for the hurt she will feel if we don't live up to her expectations afterwards. Are we ready, at the very minimum, to just do the nice things? A phone call. Flowers. Certainly, cuddling, talking. If we miss all of this completely, are we prepared for the accusation that we used her? Or the lesser accusation, that we seduced her. If she tells her girlfriends, they will probably all agree with her that, in fact, she was seduced, is innocent of the choice to make love, and that the man who slept with her and did not call her afterwards is a creep. (How did the word 'creep' enter our lexicon to represent a man who doesn't understand the precious gift? It's not even among our short list of bad words. Interestingly, a woman can utter it, everyone knows what she means, and she still hasn't committed, even verbally, transgression enough to consign herself into the bad-girl category. The current popularity of this word is nothing less than fascinating.) If a man has been identified as a creep, it won't help him one bit to argue as if they had just played a few rounds of racquetball, or had breakfast. 'Didn't *you* enjoy it? Wasn't it *mutual*? So what's your complaint?' This sort of logic is pointless.

Generally, men understand cavalier lovemaking. And, generally, women don't.

The Big Question.

What should be done? Who should capitulate? Should a man only make love to a woman if he plans to marry her?

Well, this is impossible. We fall in love, by some estimates, three times in a hundred years. Through long stretches of our lives, we're not in love at all. But lust can slam us against the wall a thousand times in a single day. Of course we cannot wait until we're in love.

So let's say it happens. Lust rages, a woman avails herself to a man, and both agree - tacitly, of course - to make love. How, therefore, should a man behave, knowing what a woman expects from him, and knowing that her expectations don't quite mesh with his own.

Again, we can't expect a woman to think the way we think. She cannot be cavalier, frivolous, or casual about sex. She may give

James Cahill

this notion a road test - many women do - but for most, casual sex simply doesn't suit them.

First, he should be a patient, caring lover. Touch her slowly, gently, and long enough so that she's thoroughly aroused. It should not be an event where he rushes, enters her before she's ready, and simply uses her to please himself. He should hold her afterward, talk to her, and take time with her.

Second, because she's given something special, it doesn't hurt to reciprocate. Of course, be subtle here. Any business-like vulgarity will make a woman wince. Women are guardians of the sublime. They civilize us. (A recent comic strip in S.F. Chronicle had a picture of the Garden of Eden, populated only by men, and they were just sitting around burping. In heaven, an angel suggested to God, "Why don't you create something that's disgusted by these belching contests." God replied: "I'm working on it.") Sex is truly a loftier enterprise for women. Give her something that honors her dignity and makes her special. On the continuum of vulgar to sublime, choose something at the latter end. A favorite book is perfect. Tell her why you like it, why you think she might like it. And women always love flowers.

In my oafish, clueless days, a slightly older woman felt sympathy for my ineptitude. After we made love, I was, I'm embarrassed to say, reading a novel, and she said, "Listen, You can't read *now!*"

I looked at her. "What should I do?"

"Do something nice afterwards." Of course, I had no idea what to do, or why. "Nothing big. Just nice," she thought for a moment. "Ice cream," she said. "Ice cream is nice."

So. Ice cream.

Don't shirk these things. While they may feel meaningless to a man, they can mean so much to a woman. Rather than feeling vulgar and used, she will feel honored, respected, and special.

Also, you may choose not to go all the way to intercourse. You may just wish to use your hands with wizardly expertise. It's penetration that makes a woman feel vulnerable, and that a tremendous gift has been given, and finally, that makes her feel connected to you. You can avoid the problem altogether, and you both can emerge from the bedroom feeling just as wonderful. This - we'll call it effective touching - is less fraught with misunderstanding than intercourse. Less fraught, because she still might feel like she's opening herself and doing the giving, but here, the giving and receiving is more equal on both sides. (I will expand on this wizardly use of hands business shortly.)

My friend Karen told me a man could do anything he wants with his hands, but once they have intercourse, everything changes. This is when the precious gift business truly kicks in, when expectations, misunderstandings, hurt feelings, and accusations can occur. It's important that a man, if he chooses intercourse, be ready to understand what a woman has given him, and understand what is expected of him. All women expect something, and a simple 'good night' won't be enough.

Of course, don't sell your own needs short. It's okay to want sex and to pursue it. Women like sex with a caring, patient man, albeit with complications.

Woody Allen understands these complications. In one failed pick-up line, he says, "I know sex without love is an empty experience, but, as empty experiences go, it's not a bad one." Men have no problem with such empty experiences. Women, on the whole, don't care for them.

And again, don't forget, after you make love to her, hold her. Linger with her. Do it whether you're in the mood or not. Women need it and love it. After lovemaking women are most vulnerable. Give her time. Talk to her. Be sweet. Be silly. In a novel called, Sundogs, author Jim Harrison says of a male character: 'Women loved him because he was a princely dallier.'

Be a princely dallier, before and after you make love.

Dallying after lovemaking is yet another skill sadly not in the repertoire of male instinct. But it's easily learned. If you haven't been doing it, don't worry. Forgive yourself and begin. Your woman will love you for it.

How little our instincts tell us about the needs of women!

As men, our most basic impulses rush us toward intercourse, and when it's over, it's over. A man doesn't need foreplay to get an erection. A woman requires time and touching to get aroused. Slow, patient touching. And afterwards, she needs to be held. Conventional wisdom tells us that love and passion will guide our hands.

Passion, in fact, gives us the wrong information.

J   J   J

"What?" Tony said. He was staring at me.

"It just occurred to me," I said, shaken from my thoughts. "That poem, 'To His Coy Mistress.' I've been teaching it to my freshman for years. It suddenly dawned on me! Andrew Marvell will *never* get his Coy Mistress to bed. I mean, listen to these lines:

> *At my back, I always hear*
> *times winged chariot hurrying near*

and:

> *The graves a fine and private place*
> *but none I think do there embrace*

and worst of all:

> *then worms shall try*
> *thy long preserved virginity*

"Is there any chance in hell his Coy Mistress can feel swept away? Can she tell her best friend, *fate took its course!*

"Even if she doesn't barf over the worms, poor Andrew will never get the first button undone. I mean, hey, she's made up her mind already, one way or the other. So, *coy my ass!* But is he trying to terrify her into bed? Time? The grave? Worms? Maybe she is coy, but perhaps all she wants is a good excuse. He isn't giving her one! Everything he tells her will make the event *her choice, her fault.* He leaves her no option out of, as you say, bad-girl culpability.

"But if he were at this table - if Andrew Marvel were at this table right now with a Muskrat Skank in front of him - I'd say, "Andy! Buddy! If it's sex you want, and of course it is and why shouldn't it be, learn how to talk to a woman. I mean, thanks for giving me a steamy way to teach freshman what an oxymoron is, but please forget the logical arguments, lose the chariots, the graves, and please please please please please forget the worms."

Tony grinned. Then he cleared his throat, and said,

"Poor poor Andrew

Won't he ever learn to woo?"

"You just made that up?" I asked.

"Right off the fucking top of my head."

I tipped my glass.

"What's the oxymoron?" Tony asked.

"*Coy... Mistress.*"

"Ahhh..." he said. "Must've been dozing in freshman English."

I looked at him. "But what about Jason?"

"You mean, did he learn to woo?"

"No," I said. "Did the two women he slept with, you know, forgive him?"

"*Forgiveness* is your question? For not calling? They might. They may never sleep with him again, but they certainly might forgive him. Hard to say. I would guess it's a kind of qualified forgiveness."

I looked at him. "Why qualified?"

"Because," Tony said, "he can't be trusted. Like the trust game. They gave him their precious gift, and he didn't receive it as one. He let them fall to the pavement. Perhaps a man calls a woman he slept with once or twice a long while ago. He asks her out. She'll go out with him but probably, in most cases, she won't sleep with him. I've seen guys scratch their heads over this. 'She slept with me before... what's the problem?' To women, trust is a huge, huge-"

"Okay. Okay," I said. "So, did you school him?"

"Me?" Tony said. "What the hell do I know? But maybe somebody will. Which brings me - do you remember the phrase, 'heavy petting'?"

"Wait," I said. "Whatever you're about to say, please don't tell me it gets worse."

He smiled and leaned back in his chair. "Sorry."

T   T   T

Lewis **and Clark**

Keith banged Francesca.

This was whispered around my. high school.

Keith had gone to second base and now, this. I had little idea about what Keith had done to lovely Francesca, and I asked Kam what it meant. Kam, mercifully, made no allusion to the fact that I was hopelessly naive. Even the sophisticated, he perhaps understood, all begin in a similar state of innocence. It's unavoidable. He had explained the base system. Now I wanted specifics. He glanced around, then, in a lowered voice, he said, "You put your finger in her pussy and you bang the walls."

I considered this.

The word 'walls', in ninth grade, was intriguing; that a pussy could have walls, and you could bang on them. I had no idea about the anatomy of a girl, but somehow, 'bang' - a word more connected to drums, firecrackers and hammers - seemed misleading.

But what Keith had accomplished fascinated me. I imagined myself performing this very act: *banging Francesca*. I nearly went crazy contemplating it. What a sweet, magical experience Keith must have had! How could she possibly let him do such a thing? Certainly she was a slut. A girl of dubious, crumbling morality. Everyone said this, that Francesca was a slut.

Of course, such an experience wouldn't happen to me for several years. I was sadly lacking in the charm and finesse possessed by a boy like Keith. I once had the fabulous pleasure of sitting by Francesca in a typing class. I even became a bit friendly with her, and I actually heard her say to herself as she rolled a clean sheet of paper into her typewriter, "Why do guys have to *tell* everybody?"

In ninth grade, I had no answer to this excellent question. But the adolescent mind is puritanical, and the fact that these liberties she indulged in - or allowed Keith to indulge in - cast a blight on her reputation seemed to me, somehow, just.

Today, I would bless such a woman.

I would burn incense at her feet, write poetry in her honor.

Our first investigations of the other sex are so exciting that we hardly require expertise. It's more about accomplishment and adventure. The first time I held a girl in my arms and was about to kiss her, I was so thrilled that I trembled.

"Are you cold?" Connie asked. I shook my head. I was in eleventh grade. I just gotten my license and this was my first date. Connie smiled calmly, amused. She was a senior, and a woman of infinitely more experience than me. I smiled too, but I couldn't stop shaking. The entire evening - the movie, sundaes at Bob's Big Boy, and especially the drive home - I was riveted on this very moment. We stood on her front lawn. I was going to kiss her, by God, and not even the humiliation of trembling would stop me.

I even *admitted* I wasn't cold. I considered this honesty a point of bravery. She could see the Promethean struggle I was undergoing. But Connie was a delight. She didn't mock me. She didn't tease me. In fact, she smiled and waited patiently for me to rally my courage.

There on her front lawn, I held her in my arms and shook with the wonderful proximity of an actual female body pressed lusciously against me. I shivered like a man in the arctic wearing nothing but his briefs, but this would not deter me.

I said to myself: *Here goes.*

Dear God in Heaven, her lips were soft!

We said our good nights, I got back into the Volkswagen my brother loaned me for the evening and, still deliciously a-tremble, I drove home. The shaking settled into a sweet humming sensation that lasted for three days. For three blissful days, I was not body-slammed with desire whenever a female was in view. I needed nothing but food, water and air, thank you.

I had kissed Connie Blackwell.

And I wanted to tell everyone.

But the point is this: a kiss will do this the first time, and sadly, it will never do it again.

This is the Lewis and Clark phase, the thrill of pure exploration.

Several years later, I sat on a bench overlooking the ocean with Patricia, a lovely girl I met in an Existential Literature class, and she slipped her magical little hand into my pants. "What's this?" she said impishly. Much later, it occurred to me that I might have said, 'Well, my dear, if existence precedes essence, how can we truly know what anything is,' but in that instant, I could think of nothing. Her two, delicately uttered words - and her lovely hand - drove me to the brink of insanity.

Lewis and Clark.

Patricia.

What was it about her? She could simply lay her hand lightly on my stomach, and I was gone. How badly I wanted to make love to her!

And make love we did.

Oh, the mystery of women! Pure magic in their lovely bodies! I felt like a man journeying to a place, alien and strange. Nothing I'd encountered on this earth looked like this, smelled like this, or, when I was bold enough, tasted like it. I could not seem to get enough touching, exploring. In the face of my fabulous curiosity, Patricia was delightfully accommodating.

Lewis and Clark!

I don't believe I was a fraction as interesting to her, but frankly, I don't remember.

The Chinese Bean Jar.

The Chinese have a theory about married sex.

When a couple gets married, for the first year of marriage, every time they make love, they should place a bean in a jar. After that first year, every time they make love - for the rest of their lives - they should take a bean out of the jar.

The theory concludes: they will never empty the jar.

This is, perhaps, a sad but accurate account of many marriages.

Are we all doomed to infrequent, pedestrian sex after our first year together?

If so, it happens like this: We taste the first thrill of sex, that Lewis and Clark enchantment of exploring the body of our partner. We touch, taste and explore. We have sex in every position we can imagine or can learn from sex manuals. But this thrill fades. It will. It must. If nothing replaces it, our amount of lovemaking plummets. The jar is never emptied.

It needn't be this way. We can empty the jar one year, refill it on our anniversary, and empty it twice again the following year.

Why doesn't this occur? I believe most people never advance much beyond that which they learned in ninth grade. The home run is the end. Oral sex? Perhaps an inside the park homerun. The base system will not sustain us for the long haul for this simple reason: it's for beginners.

Some people, in the throes of boredom, try to recapture the Lewis and Clark thrill. They find new partners and explore new bodies. This has a certain, brief appeal. A married friend told me he had a girlfriend. A young, beautiful woman. But it shocked him to discover: "Her vagina was just like my wife's!"

What did he expect? An iPod? An oboe?

Why are we shocked to discover this? Why are we erotically curious about all women?

This aspect of the male psyche is particularly vexing to women, and it's the rare woman who has understanding or sympathy for such apparent immorality in the male of the species. And men are often made to feel guilty about this natural, cosmic programming that every straight male has been blessed with.

Not cursed.

I repeat: Blessed.

To the male psyche, women are exalted, heavenly creatures. A vagina is sacred, spiritual. According to Zorba the Greek, "If you're looking for any other paradise my poor fellow, there is none. Don't listen to what the priests tell you, there's no other!" In Brighton

Beach Memoirs by Neil Simon, a boy desperately wants a picture of a naked woman, and refers reverently to her vagina as, "The Palace of the Himalayas." The monster best seller, The Da Vinci Code, posits that the vagina is literally the Holy Grail. In a play by Alan Ball (academy award winner for the screenplay, American Beauty) entitled, All That I Will Ever Be, a male character describes oral sex as, "feeling the power of all creation fill you up until you are all creation" and "just losing yourself in the fact that you are right up there in the gate of fucking life, and you get to drink it up all you want." Samuel L. Jackson, in the opening of Pulp Fiction, refers to the vagina as "The Holyiest of Holyies."

Is a woman truly a sacred being?

Is her vagina in fact, a heavenly paradise? Or is this simply a projection of the male psyche? When a man and woman make love, does he literally enter paradise, or does he *just think* he does?

These are fascinating cosmological questions, perhaps unanswerable, but it is this sacred aspect that causes men to be curious about all women. That said, I don't believe a penis holds such a consecrated place in a woman's psyche. Does a woman also see her own vagina as sacred? She must. Why else would she feel that she gives a precious gift when she makes love? But while a self-indulgent exploration of this sacred curiosity - going from woman to woman - can be fun for a while, finally, it doesn't sustain anyone's interest. And today, it's dangerous.

There's a much better alternative.

J   J   J

"So, what's really the big deal?" I said. "Going from woman to woman. I mean, if it's just breakfast?"

Tony laughed out loud. "Bless you, James! You're listening!"

"I'm listening," I said. "I'm sitting here."

"Okay," Tony said. "Breakfast. Bacon and Eggs one day! Pancakes the next! Why shouldn't a man have an affair, if it's only breakfast. Right?"

I nodded.

"This," Tony said, "is a question of unending fascination. Remember, as the psychiatrist said, we make the mistake of thinking others see the world as we see it. This is not to simply say that we all see things differently. Rather, we assume, without question, that others see things as we do. So, while you clearly understand your 'just like breakfast' metaphor, the woman in your primary relationship, if she finds out, will think something quite different: you have just violated and shattered the sacred bond of your relationship, and, she believes that *you know this*, and that you also see your crime in an equally incriminating light. The male brain has a hard time understanding any of this."

I told Tony about Milan Kundera, and his surgeon, now turned window washer, who goes from affair to affair - torture to his young wife - but he thinks, what's the problem? This has nothing to do with my wife.

"Yes!" Tony shouted. "A logical argument. Any man would agree. What does it have to do with her? All women would disagree, some with violence. Not a single woman would even come close to understanding."

"So?" I said. "What's the answer?"

"Simply this," Tony said. "*It's your choice.* I'm sorry if that sounds lame. Your rationale will be sound to you and, even if they don't openly agree, to just about every male you know. But it will hurt your woman if she finds out. She just won't understand 'breakfast'." Tony ran a finger around the rim of his glass. "But... affairs. I'm not saying don't have them. I just think we leap into them too quickly. First, at least try this: You can take your current partner - are you listening now? - and bring your lovemaking to fabulous, lofty new heights. When the bean-removal count diminishes and cobwebs grow over the jar - this is when people have affairs, or languish into tepid complacency. Most of us remain in ninth grade, perhaps for our entire lives. We stick it in and hammer away for as long as possible. We round the base pads. We know nothing different. But there's more, plenty more to know. Your own woman can be fabulously exciting."

"What do you mean, my own woman?"

"*Anyone's* own woman," he said. "Anyone's." He thought for a moment. "My friends said every man gets tired of his woman. Even if she's perfect. That you'd want other women no matter how wonderful your wife is. But you know what?"

"What?"

"I think... if we graduate from ninth grade... we might never, ever need another woman beyond the one we have."

I thought for a moment about the state of my marriage, and about my tentative plans for the evening. "I've always heard this," I said, "usually from women: Sex is a barometer of the quality of the relationship. Is it true?"

"That's a great one," Tony said. "I used to think so."

T   T   T

How much exactly, is a good relationship necessary for good sex?

A neat little metaphor springs to mind, which comes from the wine country. I lived in Napa Valley for several years, which is home of California wines - and, to the chagrin of the French - some of the best in the world. Living there made me wonder: What is more important? Good grapes, or good wine making ability? I asked this of a tour guide I knew. His face lit up at the question. "That one comes up on most tours," he said, "and I make everyone memorize the answer." He cleared his throat. "You can make *good wine* from *good grapes*. And, you can make *bad wine* from *good grapes*. But, you can't make *good wine* from *bad grapes*."

With a simple transposition: 'you can have good sex in a good relationship. And, you can have bad sex in a good relationship. But, you can't have good sex in a bad relationship."

Is this true?

Sex *can* be a barometer of how a relationship fares. But truthfully, as logical, and poetic as the wine metaphor sounds, I don't believe it to be applicable to lovemaking. The notion arises out of a pollyannish misconception, that love will guide our hands, and without love, sex is always dull.

We're not at the mercy of something as amorphous as love. We can all be great lovers with anyone – people we love, like, or even dislike.

But there is a big difference. With someone we love, we're *inspired* to please them. We try wonderfully hard to make them happy. Thus, we can be better lovers with the people we love. And, also, their simple proximity sets us aflame. Certainly, making love with someone we're in love with is a wonderfully steamy proposition. But if we know how, even with partners we don't love, we can still be fabulous lovers.

A therapist wrote in to the NY Times:

I've been doing couples therapy and family therapy for forty years. In that time, I've yet to meet a couple heading for divorce where both parties describe their sex lives as great-to-outstanding. It's one of the first things I assess, both meeting with the couple and individually with the partners. When sex works, almost always everything can be drawn along in its wake. When it doesn't, all the connection and expansiveness in the world can go down the marital drain. — Mariah (no last name given)

Conventional wisdom tells us that a good sex can follow as a consequence of a good relationship; but in fact, if lovers are empathetic and skilled, just the opposite can be true – good sex can go a long way toward making a relationship work. Without it, even the most otherwise compatible of partners may struggle.

Being a fabulous lover, whether you're in love or not.

Begin of course with slow and gentle touching. Understanding this simple concept is so crucial that it bears repetition, and a slightly more detailed explanation. In fact, the man who understands *only* this will probably - and easily - outdistance every lover his woman has ever had before him. Put simply, women love it. The lack of it is what women complain about most. In fact, improvement in *just this one area* will, in all likelihood, have your woman running to you for lovemaking.

Skin can accept anything from the roughness of massage, to the lightest caress. Touch your arm as if you are massaging it. This is great for loosening up, or for working out a cramp, but erotically, it does little. Now, touch your arm lightly. Move your hand over your skin slowly, gently. Our skin is a wonderful, amazing organ. It breathes, sweats, senses hot and cold, and judges just how much pressure we need to pick up an egg or a barbell, and wraps us neatly. But skin is also designed to receive several types of touching. Erotic touching is slow, patient, gentle, and women love to be touched in this manner.

Practice on your lover.

Grace your fingers across her back with almost no pressure.

You almost can't go too slowly. A nice guide for the slowness of an erotic touch is the ocean. Sit at the beach or on a cliff and watch the movement of waves crashing. Even if the sea is wild, the waves huge, the water still rises and crashes with a slow, graceful patience. This should be the speed of your hand as it moves lightly over your woman's body.

As the Zen master advocates, focus on your touch. Feel the contact of your skin against hers. You are tuned to her reactions - her breathing, her body movements, any sounds she makes. Concentrate on this with all of your attention. You are giving her the slow warm-up she needs and loves.

Why this focusing of your attention, you ask. Good question! Two reasons.

A) It isn't simply your touch, but your attention she craves. Touching her while you glance around distractedly will do nothing for her.

B) Focusing alleviates the hysteria to rush ahead to penetration. Every heterosexual man is familiar with this lustful hysteria - worst in our teens and twenties - that can occur in the presence of an amorous woman. It is not our fault, and is probably, again, the result of some cosmic programming to guarantee that the species procreates and survives. Ironically, it is also the biggest impediment to pleasing a woman. Focusing on our touch truly places us on another plane, one that is calm, patient, and where we have no problem giving a woman all the slow and gentle touching she needs. It is the solution to the biggest problem in lovemaking.

Begin with places that are *not* obviously erotic. Avoid her breasts, and her vagina for the moment. You'll get to these in time. A woman's entire body is erotic. Touch her less steamy places first.

Why?

Why indeed!

We men would be quite happy if a woman placed her hand in our pants before she even said hello!

Not so with a woman. She needs a long, patient warm-up. She's like a car you care about - you must make it purr before you shift into drive. But this warm-up is infinite fun. Try a few places. Her arms, her stomach, her legs. There are no mistakes.

Your mind is not racing to the wonders that await you. You have no goal at all. You are simply focused on your touch and how she responds to it. Because you are in no hurry, she may even ask you: Touch me here now, or she may simply place your hand where she wants it. She may even say, "I want you inside me.' You are bringing her to a place where tomorrow, she can tell her best friend, "Before I knew it, there we were, swept away, because, my God, his touch was so incredible!" And she will grin dreamily over the memory.

And why shouldn't she? You made love like a wizard, and because you touched her with such patience and care, she was brought to a point where she could honestly say you seduced her. Do you have any problem with this? You shouldn't. With your skill, you have liberated her from the bad-girl burden, and enabled her to enjoy loving you without guilt. You've done her a favor. Feel very good about it.

And, you've done yourself a favor.

She'll be back. She'll want you again and again.

A first encounter, or a first few encounters with a woman is like an audition. If she's experienced and knows what good lovemaking looks and feels like, a skilled lover will get a repeat performance. A bad lover may not. But from now on, all performances will be tour de force successes.

And we're getting way ahead of ourselves.

It's not tomorrow morning yet. You are still touching her, with the patience of waves crashing in the ocean.

Touch her, lightly, gently. Move on to her thighs, her tush, her abdomen. You are in no hurry get anywhere. Touch her as if you had all the time in the world. Three miraculous things happen here:

1. You will become meditatively 'in tune' with her. As you touch her slowly and gently, focusing on her and what makes her feel good, you will grow wonderfully, amazingly calm.

2. As we said earlier, the crazed, panic stricken to rush to paradise will subside. And though your desire for actual intercourse is still there, you have mastered the desire, made it irrelevant, and you are on your way to enjoying the delicious, supremely confident experience of being a great lover.

3. This slow, patient touching feels right, feels natural. If the impetuous rush to intercourse is male instinct, then logically, slow and patient touching is a battle with male instinct. This is not the case. In fact, there is no battle at all. It feels, instead, like tapping into a *more advanced instinct*. It feels right, and easy as riding a bike. This advanced instinct exists - perhaps dormant - in all of us. Tapping into it is the key to becoming a great lover.

When you feel she's ready touch her breasts. The nipples are the most sensitive, and here you can be a bit rougher. Rub them back and forth with your fingertips. Or, she may love to have her breasts held and gently massaged with a squeezing, kneading motion. You might ask which feels better, and with luck, she'll tell you.

Remain attentive, focused, and patient. All women are different - what works for one may not for another. And if this doesn't make things difficult enough, what works for one woman, *one time*, may not work for her the next time you try it. Some women have wildly sensitive breasts. But what feels good to her during one part of the month may be irritating to her during another part.

Is all this designed to keep us from getting too confident, to prevent us from thinking we know how to do it well, every time? The complexity of women seems endless. I would ask our creator: Why did you make men so astonishingly simple to please, while women seem so vastly complex?

Are women meant to be such endless confusion?

Perhaps. But we are up to the challenge. Touch her breasts. If she enjoys it, kiss them. Move your tongue back and forth over her nipples. Again, a bit of roughness is okay. Spend some time here. She will probably love this. Or, she may prefer your hand. Again, you can ask her. But she may feel too shy for this. If so, attend to her reactions - her breathing, her heartbeat, any sounds she makes. What of her other body language? Is she luxuriating in your touch? Is she focusing on where you touch her? Remember, her whole body is an erogenous zone. So, continue to touch her in a variety of places.

And kiss her lips. Her mouth has an interesting, direct connection with her vagina. *Ignite one pair of lips and inflame them all!* Take your time kissing. Be gentle here too. Light, slow, gentle. No tongue jamming. Play with her lips, with her tongue. And consider, with a bit of pride, that at this very moment, down below - where the most fascinating wonders in the universe occur - she's getting wetter and wetter.

The fires of a woman are stoked indirectly!

This is one of the four pillars of wisdom, and the other three are irrelevant.

Touch her stomach; slowly, gently. Her thighs; slowly, gently.

Lightly touch her inner thighs. Then, grace your fingers lightly over her vagina. Do this for a bit. No hurry, no particular goal. Then, with your finger, gently check if she's wet. If she is - don't touch her there before she's wet - then gently touch her vagina. Grace your fingers lightly over the outer lips. Lightly, gently, slowly, touch her inside.

Do this with excruciating slowness.

She may utter a slight, delightful gasp. Of course, this means you are a stunningly good lover. Enjoy the compliment. You didn't rush to get here - no wonder she gasped. But now that you're here - and her attention is focused on the slightest movement of your fingers - you're still in no rush. She's hot and wet and ready and dying for what you are about to do next.

Still, you are in no hurry.

Not at all.

You are still focused completely upon her.

James Cahill

Consider: You are now in contact with her most precious, secret, private place. And from her point of view, this place is a sacred gift. Her state of mind now, is one of giving, of generosity. And this special gift, she has chosen to bequeath to you. YOU, my friend! You shiver with honor, with gratitude. This is where she is most vulnerable, most sensitive, softest. How good she feels on your fingertips! And this is where you will be *particularly* slow, *especially* gentle.

This is her gift to you.

Appreciate it as a mystical gift from the gods, which, in fact, it is.

Touch her here with extreme gentleness, the outer lips, and then, the inner lips. For now, touch her here just on the outside. Then, slowly, place one finger barely inside and bring it up to her clitoris. This is where the two inner lips converge at the top of her vagina. This tiny organ is wildly sensitive, and the way to touch it properly has baffled every man since he first ventured a hand to this miraculous bit of Heaven.

Here, again, as if to keep us off-balance and baffled, the needs of all women are different. In the Kurt Vonnegut novel, Breakfast of Champions, a character is about to have a tryst with a woman and his primary concern is this: *not to pay too much attention to her clitoris.* He knows a woman needs to be touched here, but too much and the place gets irritated. Any man concerned about the pleasure he gives his women has struggled mightily with this question: how much attention do you give a clitoris without irritating it?

You will never have this problem again.

There is a way to touch a clitoris that ends all guesswork. With many women, it will be fabulously successful. (If not, don't worry, there are other possibilities and we'll get to them.) First, dip a finger down, inside, where it's steamy and wet. Always keep your finger wet. Bring a bit of this natural lubricant up with your finger - whoever designed this wonderful place thought of everything - and move it very lightly, over this tiny, seemingly insignificant bump. *Very* slowly, *very* lightly, *very* gently, with your finger, describe a tiny circle over it. Up one side, over the top, down the other side. Slowly, gently, patiently. Underneath, up again. Do it so lightly, that you can't believe you've ever done *anything* so lightly, so delicately.

Focus your attention here.

She will begin to breathe harder. The male instinct (which you have abandoned) is to now rub harder, faster.

But no. You, the maestro, are too skilled for such barbarianism. In fact, you do just the opposite. Dip your finger again, down where it's magical, slippery and wet. Continue to move it over the clitoris, but now, go even lighter, even more slowly. What is a good barometer for how lightly to touch her here? Consider: nearly all women love oral sex. The reason is that nothing is as soft as a tongue. So make your finger as soft, delicate, and tongue-like as possible. It's extremely important to keep her clitoris wet. If she doesn't get particularly wet, a few drops of a water based lubricant works amazingly well. There are plenty of lubricants in the family planning section of any drug store. Oil based lubricants can dissolve condoms and stain bed sheets. If a condom is on the agenda use a water-based lubricant. Regardless, keep a small, plastic bottle by the bed.

So. You are almost barely touching her!

This is so fascinatingly antithetical to what our instincts tell us, but try it. Slower, gentler. And you are now about to experience one very important aspect of understanding women.

We don't *drive* a woman to an orgasm.

We lead her there, slowly, gently, lightly, without any coercion, and wait patiently until she *falls* into it.

She will breathe harder, and harder. Continue, slowly, lightly. Not pressing down. Not rubbing. Barely touch her.

She will probably come.

She may explode with shouts and shake and contort violently in your arms. She may simply turn her head to one side and utter a sweetly cultured, "Oh!" She may compliment you.

No one has ever touched her like this before.

Enjoy the compliment. You have done well.

J   J   J

"Give me your hand," Tony said. He reached across the table.

"Huh?"

"Just give me your hand."

Tentatively, I put my hand on the table.

"Okay. Now, this third knuckle." He held my hand and looked at me. "Pretend this is a clitoris."

"*What!*" I glanced around. "*Jesus!* Tony-"

"Relax," he said.

"Do you have to hold my hand?" I looked around again. A woman at another table looked over, briefly.

"I said *relax*," he said with a grin.

I tried to relax. But this was weird. A clitoris on the back of my hand. Then he touched my knuckle with his finger. "Tony, Christ! Could you hurry at least? People are-"

"What do you care?" He said. "I'll be done in a second. Now, most men think you touch a clitoris like this." He mashed down on my knuckle and rubbed.

I glanced around. A woman at another table eyed us. Now she stared shamelessly. Oh, God.

"But the way to do it is, to keep your finger wet," he dipped a finger in his beer, "and do it like this." He reached between my fingers, then back to my knuckle - very slowly, very lightly.

I didn't want to look at the woman. I'm certain she was mesmerized. I'm sure she overheard.

"Okay! Okay," I said, pulling my hand away. "I got it."

Tony was laughing. "What's wrong? What's the big-?"

"Jesus!" I said, glancing around again. The woman was looking down at a salad and trying to keep from grinning. "I think she heard you!"

"Really?" Tony looked at her with interest. "Good. Maybe I can ask her for a few pointers-"

"No!" I said. "Ask her nothing. Please."

He grinned. He got up, but thankfully, to use the restroom. He wasn't going to ask the woman anything. But he would have. If I didn't stop him, he certainly would have. That's the problem with guys like Tony. They play by a different set of rules.

So.

Tony had just explained, verbally and graphically, how to touch a clitoris. He figured all of this out, because he loves problems. I recalled once, when the accelerator cable broke on his Volkswagen. He couldn't use his gas pedal, and in the backseat, there was nothing but a coat hanger and a rope, and, far as I could tell, we were stranded. I saw the problem solver's gleam in his eyes. He propped open the hood and held it in place with the coat hanger. He then figured a way to hook the rope to the engine, and ran it along the side of the car and through the driver's side window, which he just pulled on to give it gas, and off we went, cruising down the highway, laughing like fools. He drove around like this for months. Tony's mechanic was amazed when he finally brought it in. This was Tony. And I imagined the same gleam in his eyes as he scratched his head over this clitoral conundrum.

And while I thought about this, about Tony's lack of modesty, and about what I'd been doing wrong my entire life, I was thinking: My wife, Cindy. My sizzling department secretary, Maureen. My trying-to-keep-from-grinning-but-failing-miserably woman at the next table with the salad. My agonizing slip of a waitress. In my mind, I was loving them all, each individually, one after the other. And my hands were safely hidden below the table... practicing... practicing... so light... so slow.

And Tony returned.

T   T   T

Consider this business of leading her gently, this falling into an orgasm. It seems to explain so much about women. Don't muscle. *Finesse.* Just light touching, and let it happen. Is it male instinct that makes us so effortful, so impatient? Is it the dogged, Judeo-Christian work ethic, or some myth that women love a strong, persistent man? That they melt at the power of his passion? Such nonsense clearly sets us on the wrong path.

Not only does a woman love your touch in bed, she craves it all day. At any given moment, run your fingers gently down her back. If she is beside you at a party, and you're speaking to a friend, put your arm around her. Touch her. Caress her. Hold her hand. Grace your fingers along her arm.

Don't fight these requirements: touching lightly, gently, in and out of bed. They're fun. Enjoy them. She will look forward to climbing into bed with you. She will reward you a thousand-fold.

If you didn't know this before, don't fret over it.

None of this is discussed. We are given no pamphlet, no course, no seminar in how to make love to a woman. We get our knowledge from surreptitious whispering. We extrapolate misinformation from jokes. Little dick jokes, and even lust itself is ridiculed.

Joe can't keep his zipper up!

Ah ha ha ha ha!

Mark'll fuck anything that moves!

Heh heh heh heh heh!

What do such jokes tell us? That we must be needless, yet, when called upon, we must be in possession of an erection that is eternal and extends from here to Botswana. Certainly, they preclude the possibility of revealing our innocence, of asking questions, of sharing serious advice. So we go it alone. We do our best in isolation. Very few people are safe to ask. It's important to understand this male-to-male ridicule. It inspires a pose of sexual prowess, creates an atmosphere where any man would be terrified to reveal his innocence.

So how do we learn?

Women are unable to tell us.

Our instincts leave us oblivious.

Regarding sex and men, Earnest Hemingway wrote: "...all the equipment you will ever have is provided and each man learns all there is for him to know about it without advice; and it makes no difference where you live."

J   J   J

"Do you know the capital of Florida?" Tony asked me.

I shook my head.

"Ever read any porn?"

"Who hasn't?"

He smiled.

"Don't stop, Tony. We're just getting warmed up. *Do I like backgammon?* I hate it! *Do I brush twice a day?* Not only twice, but up and down! *Do I talk to my plants?* I did once and felt like an idiot! Do I want to hear that it's even more complicated? No, I don't."

"It is and it isn't," he said. "Most of these things, once you start, feel natural. They're all easy. But this last bit - which also feels easy once you get going - was the toughest part of all to understand." He picked up a ketchup-soggy French fry. He contemplated it, replaced it on his plate, and wiped his hands on a napkin. "One last question. When you make love to Cindy. Do you talk?"

I thought: Did I talk to my wife when I made love to her? Was this too intrusive? Perhaps. But, I was sitting across the table from Mr. Intrusive himself.

I shook my head. "Never. What's there to talk about?"

"Has she asked you to?"

I thought about this. "As a matter of fact, early on, she did. Why? Do you talk when you make love?"

"I didn't used to," Tony said. "I certainly didn't use to."

T   T   T

Talk to me!

How I had suffered that impossible request! How many women had uttered it and left me baffled, stunned to the core with feelings of incompetence? How often had it left me ready to slit my own throat?

Talk to me!

How can anyone make such a demand, and then... *just lay there?*

Just lay there, as if to say, *let the show begin!*

Lovemaking! What kind of circus was this?

Hands, mouth, tongue, everything going, *keep that thing perky*, touch her stomach, touch her back, touch her thighs, and *keep that thing perky*, kiss her neck, kiss her lips, too much tongue? Not enough tongue? Don't forget to *keep that thing perky*, and that clit, don't forget the clit, is it time to touch it or not? Is she wet? Is she dry? How much touching is enough? Too hard? Too light? How much is too much? Is she ready or not, and *keep that thing perky perky perky*, because if the prelude goes to quickly, by God, I'll hear about it, the bad progress report will arrive and even if it doesn't, I'll know, *perky perky perky*, but don't detonate too soon, or by God, I'll hear about that too! Getting too excited? Whoa! Think about baseball, calm down, calm down, and don't forget ears, lick lick lick those ears, Christ, I damn near forgot the ears, and breasts and *keep that thing perky* and, don't supernova too soon because then all hell will surely break loose, I've certainly suffered that one, legs-feet-arms-back-tush-breasts-ears, and then, only then, when I think and hope and pray I've done everything and I'm clear of blame, ineptitude and oafishness, and I can just relax and try to maybe enjoy at least a bit of this madness, then, out of the blue, out of God knows where, undoubtedly out of some insidious prompt from the sisterhood of the damned, she says those three pernicious little words: *Talk to me.*

And in addition to *all* of this - hands tongue mouth breasts feet *perky perky perky* - on top of everything, *I'm supposed to keep up a running monologue?*

My dear.

My sweet wonder of a woman. You, who have blessed a poor soul like me, graced me with your stunning nakedness - I beg of you: *Ask me a question.*

I shall be delighted to answer.

Start a conversation.

I will happily pick up its thread.

Toss out a topic.

I shall pontificate with delight.

But what am I to make of this cheeky, ill bred, downright rude, and utterly baffling request?

But the request was so consistent among women, so infuriating, and so suggestive of some horrendous inability on my part as a lover, that I, of course, began to argue. I argued in a way that I thought was logical and clever. Once, when a woman named Gina made this obnoxious request...

No. Forgive me. To be fair, there was not the slightest bit of obnoxiousness about it. In fact, there never is. In truth, my lover snuggled comfortably against me and said, with delicious, breathy sweetness: "Talk to me." Then she snuggled again, ready to listen.

Her request inspired only blankness, exasperation, and finally, the smartass in me. I said, "Tallahassee is the capital of Florida."

She emitted some incoherent noise of disgust.

"You said 'talk to me'," I said, now fuming, as this woman unearthed the ugly truth about what a sub-par lover I actually was. "I talked."

Her exhale of hopelessness stung me.

I now spoke slowly, teeth gritting, but with the patience of a Buddha. "What would you like me to talk *about?*"

"Anything," she said Anything! I began to sweat. I said calmly, patiently, "Didn't I talk about *anything?*"

"Tallahassee is the capital of Florida?"

I nearly let go an extended scream at the top of my lungs.

Women! What do they want? Even if you ask them, they won't tell you! That I was an inept lover was irritating enough. That she would tell me nothing, even when I asked - concerned, sensitive man that I was - drove me half insane.

Then the epiphany occurred, the sea change came; the fifteen minutes where Mr. No-Patience, Mr. Nothing-But-Rushed-Guesswork died a happy death. I stopped arguing. My perplexity was gone, my feeling of touchy ineptitude fled. In fact, women never even mentioned those three miserable words again.

Why?

Why indeed!

Because I began to talk endlessly! I spoke nonsense. I flirted. I teased her. I gave her guided tours of her own body. I made up stories with my lover as the heroine! I spoke with shocking but tasteful crudeness that made her blanch. I told her my fantasies about her. If I had none, I invented them!

Once I began, it was easy! Not difficult at all!

James Cahill

A friend, Janine, told me of a dazzling lover she had - Jeffrey - a boyfriend of several years. Of course, I asked her what made him a great lover.

"He talks to me," she said, simply.

Flattering for Jeffrey certainly. But still baffling. Does a man care if his woman talks to him during sex? Not in the slightest! But I was getting a sense of what it meant for women.

"Have any other lovers talked to you?" I asked.

She hesitated a minute, as if combing her memory of a vast population of rabid suitors, then replied, quietly, "No."

"And that was all?" I asked. "That was the only thing, *special*, that he did? Talk to you?"

She nodded. I was fascinated.

It truly sounded like her Jeffrey had done nothing - no gymnastics, no reverse back flips, no death defying half gainers onto the mattress. He used no ice cream, no elaborate tongue parries, no Baryshnakovian leaps or spins. Certainly no dexterity with a repertoire of positions. In fact, if he displayed any particular physical skill at all - which he apparently didn't - it was irrelevant to Janine.

And no one else had talked to her. How many men had failed her on this key point? Who could tell? But all of them - perhaps, vast hordes of lovers, queuing up around the globe sixteen times - had loved her in complete silence.

Women. Once you begin to understand them, so much *else* about them becomes clear.

J   J   J

"James! Colleague in this bottomless mystery! Pay attention here!"

"I'm listening!"

"What do you think a woman wants when she asks you to talk to her?"

"God only knows!"

T   T   T

She simply wants connection.

This is why 'Tallahassee is the capital of Florida' - as if I couldn't guess - was such a crashing failure. My woman wanted to know I was with her in spirit as well as body. It's not a time for useless facts or world issues, or anything, in fact, that doesn't concern her directly. It's certainly not a time to be a smart aleck. Remember, she has just bequeathed to you her single, most precious gift. This is why she feels justified in making what seems, to the male ear, such a strange demand. But you won't panic in the face of such a challenge. Just share a thought you had about her recently - that very day in fact. Tell her something she wore really looked incredible. You even want her to wear it next time you go out. Tell her the way her hair falls in her face really looks sexy. Then pull her hair over her face. Tell her you were thinking about something she said. Tell her what it was, and the thought it inspired. Ask her how she keeps her skin so smooth.

Get silly. Women are wonderfully emotional creatures. Silliness, goofiness - diffuses the heaviness they may feel as a result of what can be the sheer terror of being naked and sexual. Once she's given herself to you, she is frighteningly vulnerable. Your behavior at this moment is crucial. What you do now will either make her feel sublime as a goddess or as wretched and irrelevant as road-kill. Women need your words like they need your slow and gentle touch. Don't argue; don't say you're not a talker. Just do it. Like slow and gentle touching, once you begin; once you dip your toe into the water, you'll want to dive into the raging current. Go without a life preserver. Give her the connection she wants. Ask about her dreams, tell her yours. If you don't know her favorite color, find out.

If she likes you and she is about to make love to you, if you're in the midst of lovemaking, or you're winding things up or down, she's vulnerable. She needs to hear your voice. She's given

you a gift whether you know it or not. Reciprocate. Your voice
will liberate her from the guilt that's ready and waiting to pounce
on her with two, clawed feet. Your words will make her feel safe
and finally, get her hotter than your hands ever can. The door
to her sexuality is her emotions. The key to her emotions is your
voice.

And this, ultimately, is the realm of loftier lovemaking. And
this is why so many people experience sex for the first time and
think, 'so that was it? That's what all the fuss is about?'

No. The fuss is about something much, much better.

There is more.

Man. Woman.

Two halves, connecting into one miraculous, synergistic whole.
Biologically. Spiritually. But consider: A physical connection that
transcends the physical. Selfishness frustrates the connection.
Impatience subverts it. We must tune in to our partners and surrender to them. A woman can only surrender if she feels safe. We can
help her feel safe with our patience and our voice. Only then can the
magic occur.

This is what the fuss is about. In fact, in this new universe of lovemaking, what was a home run (intercourse) is now
more like first base. It's but a starting point in a skilled lover's
evolution.

Because of this precious gift a woman gives, the guilt she may
feel, and her deep emotional vulnerability, keep your talk light,
even impish. Hold her. Feel compassion for this mystical, illogical,
emotional creature. What a precious package she is! Understand the
heaviness this moment could turn into. Know how she trusts you
with her gift, her vulnerability.

Lighten things up. Help her relax.

Tell her how beautiful her breasts are. 'But which one do I like
better? This one is quite lovely. (Kiss it.) However, this one has it's
own infinitely magical qualities. (Kiss this one, lingeringly.) But if I
kiss this one too long, will that one become jealous? Why can't they
get along? Do they always fight like this?

"And such a tush! It's a wonder men don't line up for miles just for a mere glimpse." Imagine a woman, naked, nervous, insecure, listening to such nonsense. Of course she'll relax.

Or tell her, "I had a fantasy about you. Would you like to hear it?"

What woman - lying in bed with you - will say, "No, I don't, thank you, and frankly, I find the whole idea disgusting." Not many. They love to lay silently in the safety of your arms as you tell them, in essence, how desirable they are.

J   J   J

"Why fantasies?"

"Well, fantasies," Tony said. "It doesn't *have* to be fantasies. But she just wants you to make her feel desirable."

"*Desirable?*" I said. "You're *sleeping* with her, for Godsake! What more information does she-"

"Maybe it's something like this," Tony said. "Have you ever had woman tell you, 'I feel so *safe* with you.'?"

I nodded. Cindy has told me this.

"It feels good," he said. "It makes you feel like a man. *We* need to feel competent; *they* need to feel safe and desirable. Well, they need to feel competent too. But women generally aren't quite so crazed about competence as we are."

I thought for a moment. I took a long breath.

"Listen," Tony said. "It's not so daunting. It seems that way, but once you try it - talking - it's easy. In fact, the more silliness, the more goofiness and nonsense, the better. Nothing is more fun. You're making her feel safe, desirable, and *hot*. And I promise you; she'll be back again and again. The first time might be like jumping off a high dive. Just take the risk."

The risk, I thought. Your hands, your voice, your imagination. All you need to get a woman as hot as possible. Which pretty much summed up my blossoming agenda for the evening.

"The better the arousal, the better the detonation," Tony said. "Words, even alone, can take a partner across the galaxy."

"That's why you asked about porn."

"Mere words can create an actual, physical reaction. The right words. It amazes me. Don't be crude, of course. Be tastefully erotic. What a gift to give a lover! Bring her to a dazzling supernova that lights up the firmament!"

"Sex is good," I said intelligently.

"Truer words, my friend, were never spoken. Babies who aren't held have a multitude of problems - *including death*. Married people live longer than the unmarried. Sex improves the immune system and much good research supports this. I can vouch for its help in stress relief. It's a magical sleep aid. Unrequited lust, I'm certain, will soon be identified as a precursor to cancer, heart disease, Alzheimer's, shortened life span, bad skin, lower IQ, and twenty-seven major illnesses. The necessity of hot, sweet passion in our lives will soon be recognized. Then, booths will appear everywhere. *Love Booths*. In a Love Booth, anyone can get the relief they need safely, via an expert's touch. And at shockingly affordable prices: $5.00 a visit! Insurance will cover twenty visits per month. What do you think?"

My thoughts: Was this drought with Cindy a precursor to Alzheimer's? Would I spend my twilight years oblivious and drooling due to not enough sex with my wife?

"Love booths," I said. "Tony, you're a true visionary. I'd always suspected it, but now-"

"I knew you'd think so."

"But tell me," I said. "What do women need to know about us? Have you thought about it?"

"I have." He nodded, finished his beer and said, "But first, consider this situation: A man is out with his wife. Someplace where beautiful women abound. He looks at them, the beautiful women. What happens?"

"She gets angry," I said, fidgeting uncomfortably. I wondered, *why this?*

"You too?" he looked at me, grinning, obviously reading my thoughts. "I had this very problem with Jenny! I was infallibly loyal, but if I looked at another woman, it was equal to committing an infidelity. A *visual* infidelity. It's the perfect problem!"

"The perfect problem? I could stand a bit less perfection in my-"

"Women!" Tony said, his voice devout. "I don't claim to understand them, but dear God in Heaven, I love the way they look. The way they smell! I love their endless allure and mystery. How can anyone tell me *not to look at women?*"

Thank you, I thought. I did not want, yet another lecture about what a despicable bastard I was. How I was the perfect vulgarian. How the women I looked at didn't even look like Cindy, so there was *proof* that I was cheating, in my mind.

"What do you mean, 'the perfect problem?'" I said.

T   T   T

What women need to know.

I took a poll.

I asked several women, how often, at most, they liked to make love in a week. Their answers hovered from one to four times. There were many twos but several said, "At most, three times a week."

I put the same question to men. Most said they would like to make love seven to fourteen times a week. There were quite a few 'tens'. The answers were consistent, and, interestingly, so was the language. Several men responded, "Twice a day would do me just fine."

Aside from the number, what does this, "do me just fine" mean? It means this: If a man could make love twice a day, the agony of lust would be abated. The irritating, minute-by-minute distracting urge would be gone.

Woody Allen had some cinematic fun with this lopsided desire. In a wonderful scene from Annie Hall, Woody and Annie are both, separately, in therapy. A split screen is used and they are both asked the same questions.

James Cahill

> Alvy's psychiatrist: How often do you sleep together?
> Annie's psychiatrist: Do you have sex often?
> Alfy: Hardly ever. Maybe three times a week.
> Annie: Constantly! I'd say three times a week.

The first thing a women should know about her man is this: While her sexual need ebbs and rages at different times during the month, a man's lust is often a constant, oppressive, unrequested nightmare. It's particularly important for a woman to understand one other simple fact: While lovemaking adds to a woman's pleasure in life, for a man, while it also adds to his pleasure, mostly, it relieves his misery.

For a man, sex is relief.

This is why there are female prostitutes for men, and not vice versa. The agony can be so intense that a man will pay money to have it alleviated. Perhaps a woman can understand this 'relief from misery' situation during those post-menstrual periods where her desire climbs, but who can say what truly compares? Probably, most women just have to accept an intellectual understanding of this; I doubt if they can truly feel it. And for the courageous woman who tries to understand what it's like to have a penis, even if she can imagine the thrill of penetrating a woman, I'm not sure she could ever grasp the rest of it, which is lust, constant and oppressive.

For woman, a concept so foreign is difficult to comprehend, but if the notion is taken on faith, I believe it can be understood. Typically, lust can rage constantly in a man, and women should try to have compassion for this. Many times, I've heard the following statement, uttered in a sneering, disgusted tone, "Men are so *visually stimulated!*"

It's true. We are. And women are *visually stimulating.* Consider breasts; they enter the room before the woman herself! Shapely hips. *Look at us,* they scream. Tight sweaters. Attractive legs. And some women wake up three hours early just to get ready.

Why?

To rivet our poor, helpless attention. Women are not only designed to make us look at them but spend fortunes on the enterprise. Cosmetics are one of our greatest expenses in America. More than cars, more than houses, more than cancer research, more than we spend to help third world countries. In fact, our cosmetic budget is more than our education budget, and nearly half our military budget. We want to attract people more than we want to educate them, and half as much as we want to blow them to oblivion.

Men don't stand a chance.

Suffice to say, if a man and a woman sit together in a coffee shop, and his gaze leaves her for a moment and drifts to a pretty woman ordering a latte at the counter, she shouldn't trouble herself over it. If having sex with another woman, from a man's point of view, is like breakfast, then what is looking at another woman? Coffee? Not even coffee. One lump of sugar. Half a lump, and she will be forgotten in minutes. But a woman who does not understand this may mistakenly view his gaze upon another woman as tantamount to a horrendous breach in the sanctity of her union with him. She believes men see the world as she herself sees it. Because if *she* were to look at a man the way he just looked at that lovely girl ordering a latte, there might, indeed, be a breach in the sanctity of the relationship.

There is no breach. This is what women need to understand.

J   J   J

We called for a third pint, and Tony twisted his back, eliciting a few audible pops, then exhaled, shook his head and looked at me.

T   T   T

My own girlfriend once said she didn't like the way I looked at other women. I had no idea I was looking - certainly not in a way that bothered her. I explained the problem to a friend. He laughed knowingly, and answered in one word: 'discretion.'

I began to watch other men in the presence of their wife or girlfriend, and then, suddenly, in the presence of a fabulously attractive woman. Instantly, I understood the word discretion. It's a quick, one second glance, and then back to whatever it was he was doing. What occurred in that second? Did the man convert his brief snapshot to an indelible memory, the sweetness of which he could study in the privacy of his own mind; a place where no one could bother him? I tried this. One second was hardly enough; for some beauties, it was nowhere near enough, but it kept the peace.

Discretion.

Again, in other cultures people respond differently. I explained the situation to a West African woman. Her name was Emileen, and she told me, "If the woman is beautiful, of course he should look at her! He and his wife or girlfriend can even have a conversion about how beautiful she is!"

But rather than take sides, it's infinitely more interesting to simply wonder why men and women are designed this way. Why are men so visually stimulated? Why are women so visually stimulating, and why do they put so much money and effort into being beautiful and desirable? Why does lust rage in men so frequently and mercilessly, while in women, it is, comparatively less frequent? Why are our needs set up so differently?

Why this tension rather than harmony?

Understanding this tension is the key to leaving the realm of pedestrian, round-the-base-pads sex and entering a domain of otherworldly lovemaking. Men and women must both begin by working to extend their gender-centric understanding in order to accept, embrace and finally celebrate the astounding strangeness of the opposite sex. As a man tries to understand and meet the needs of his woman - so different than his own - she should try to understand his struggle with lust, constant and oppressive, and love him frequently and with gusto.

How my life flows; how productive and relaxed I am when my sex life is humming. Though other women are still not one increment less beautiful, I don't desire them nearly as much. I have no desire to 'screw everything in sight.' Once I understood this 'precious gift' business, women began to look different to me. The gift of their sexuality seemed too special to simply love them and run. But the desire to 'screw everything in sight' is real and familiar to most men. More than once, I've seen women shocked as I explained that a man could sleep with her and feel absolutely nothing in the way of an emotional connection. And *her* reaction - pure disbelief - shocks me.

I was discussing this with a good friend named Betty. I told her a man could have sex with a succession of women with no problem.

"I've heard this," she said.

"Do you understand it?"

She shook her head.

"But this is how we are," I said, and because I knew she was religious and I wanted to hear her reaction, I added, "and programmed this way by the Almighty."

She laughed. "I hardly believe that!"

I laughed too, and it was time to change topics. Women, it seems, not only don't understand the information but also don't like it. Their connection to sexuality is deeply emotional, connected to the loftier realms of love, art, and religion. From such a vantage point, an honest male perspective seems hideously vulgar. It isn't. A male worldview is equally sacred.

Some women may understand this difference as an advantage. Meaning: because men are less connected emotionally to sex, they have a kind of power over women - a man can have sex with a woman and dismiss her. But is this an advantage? I don't think so. If a woman has such a readily physical and emotional experience when she makes love, then her experience with sex is truly more profound than his. If this is true, and it seems to be, well, I'm jealous. Further, a constant and oppressive lust is much more of a burden than an advantage. It could easily be argued that the edge goes to the lover with the more tempered desire – usually but not always the woman - as this grants her a greater ability to set limits, or, to choose this or that mate, and whether or not to make love in the first place.

When viewed from a gender-centric perspective, with no attempt to leap across the abyss, the subject irks everyone. Men feel unnecessarily criticized for something their very nature impels them toward, and women feel angry that men can be so indiscriminate when it comes to something so profound as lovemaking.

It needn't be such a battlefield.

James Cahill

Infidelity revisited.

When a man is not pleasing his lover, and she may consequent-ly be pushing him away, he is more apt to go afield and find other lovers, to recapture a feeling of prowess and competence. However, when he actually *is* competent - when he knows how to please his lover – she becomes a more willing, enthusiastic partner, and he doesn't need other women. Certainly not as much. He is quite happy to witness his woman finding joy in his touch and his voice.

While a man needs to learn to please his woman, women also must learn a few simple things: Don't send your man into the world in a state of carnal agony. And never use sex as a bargaining chip. When a man does not know how to effectively please a woman, because she receives sporadic or no pleasure, sex for her can take the form of a favor. She may reward him for helping with the house-work, or deny him for leaving a mess in the kitchen. But when a couple shares in reciprocal and effective pleasure-giving, lovemak-ing truly becomes a sacred act, separate from the thousand struggles both face each day. Both will crave that time together, regardless of the state of the kitchen. How I hate it when I hear so-called sex experts say, "Housework is the best foreplay." They suggest this as a cute bit of bartering. She's not getting any pleasure so she might as well get the living room vacuumed. Of course, a man should do his share of the housework, but making sex contingent on favors or behavior sets up a horrible paradigm. The bargain should rather be for pleasure given and received by each person.

A very brief, tiny history of human sexuality.

Pleasing a woman is complicated for a man to understand, and its methods are not readily obvious. A woman who does not get her needs met or finds sex painful becomes a reluctant lover. This is a serious problem for a man whose sex drive is constant and oppressive.

How has this problem been solved in the past?

One solution? Subjugate women. Deny them earning power so they must depend on a man and provide sex in order to live. If she wanted to eat, she had to put out. Female subjugation is one of many disappointing consequences of the serious problem of bad sex, or, more specifically, sex that does not please women.

Enter: the 1960's.

Women burned their bras and demanded equal rights and earning power. They received them (for the most part) and are now filling universities and taking high paying jobs to support themselves. A liberated woman is not dependent on a man to live, and consequently, she can say no to sex. So we have gone from bad sex to no sex. A sexless marriage is sadly is quite common.

Is there a better way to solve this problem?

Is there a next phase to our sexual evolution?

The next phase might be this: Women will make love because they love sex, because their men are experts at giving them pleasure. There will be no bartering of sex for favors; just two people pleasing each other intensely and frequently because they're both good at it and it feels wonderful. When a man successfully pleases his woman, there is no need to subjugate her in order to get the sex he needs. She will make love to him willingly and enthusiastically.

But what happens when a man reaches amorously for his lover and, for whatever reason, he frequently hears the word, "No."

Such a man goes out into the world in carnal agony.

Of course his desire is to be loyal, but there are plenty of other women out there, single and married, some with dubious ethical codes. Cheating occurs, and the statistics - with questionable veracity - conclude that more than half of the married men polled had cheated, whereas only a few of the women had. Of course, this begs the question as to who admits what, but still, there it is. Why so much cheating? And how do we prevent it? We can't follow each other around. And it's poisoning to a relationship to interrogate a partner about what he or she did each day, and to whom they spoke.

I had a partner who used to question me frequently on this score. If I had spoken to a woman, I found myself unconsciously concocting stories about what a bitch the woman was. Once my girlfriend questioned me about a woman I'd happened to speak to that day. I left the discussion at that: I had spoken to her. My girlfriend waited a bit, then said, "Well?"

"Well what?"

"Tell me what a bitch she is."

It stunned me when I realized the pattern we had fallen into. I could think of nothing in the woman's character to convey a sense of her bitchiness.

In retrospect, we were both ignorant, abysmal lovers. The Lewis and Clark thrill had died long ago. Our lovemaking had plummeted to roughly an obligatory once a week. I don't recall if she was leveraging sex for favors, but I often heard the word, 'No." I raged with lust, and consequently, the rest of the women in the world seemed to sparkle with sexuality. I looked at other women. It made her crazy. It made her wildly suspicious.

I blame no one.

Now, I understand the need for reciprocal understanding and generosity. Men need to be generous with their patience, with knowing how a woman would like to be touched. Women also need to be generous.

The word 'generous' implies doing things for another that may not immediately seem pleasing to us, and this raises an obvious question. If men want sex seven to fourteen times a week, and women only two to four (though much of this lopsided desire can easily be evened up with more enlightened lovemaking) how can a woman keep her man happy, keep the rest of the women in his life from crackling with sexuality, and not feel as if she's having sex when she doesn't want to?

The answer is breathtakingly simple. Ladies, get some lotion or lubricant and employ the sweet loving grace of your hands. Lie by his side, sit beside him, or sit between his legs. If you wish to give the Rolls Royce treatment, one hand on his penis, one massages his balls.

How is this done? Simply move your hand up and down over his penis until he comes. The end is the most sensitive. Use a pulling motion. Ask him how he likes it. He will probably be happy to tell you. He may be too shy.

Male friends have confided their shock at how many women don't have the slightest idea as to how to touch a man. Some women, of course, can work pure magic with their hands. But many aren't so adept, and I say this, of course, after talking extensively about the fact that men are just as ignorant about how to touch a women.

A friend told me he briefly dated a woman who had been divorced after twenty years of marriage. She touched him with this odd, squeezing motion that was not pleasurable in the least. Twenty years of marriage, and I could imagine the silence that must have pervaded the lives of this couple, to result in such unsatisfying touching. Most people will not admit to naiveté but, in fact, it's quite prevalent. Certainly we all begin in a state of ignorance. Reticence regarding sex, shyness, a pose at wide experience, the mockery one might face in asking an innocent question - even the embarrassment of going to the sexuality section of the bookstore - these all prevent men and women from learning what they need to know about how to please each other. When I attended college, in an off-campus store, I witnessed three female students sneaking a look at a women's oriented pornographic magazine. I glanced over as they flipped through picture after picture of naked men, and I heard one young lady ask, "How does he make it so straight?"

I hope her friends enlightened her.

So, as a woman massages her man, she should pay attention to him - his breathing, his heartbeat, and his moans of ecstasy for which she may feel happily responsible. As she touches him, she should try different pressures, learn what he likes.

And talk to him. Don't be shy here. She should make this fun for herself, too. She can be impish, erotically goofy. "What's this?" she might gasp, and he will love it. Of course, she can say what she wishes, as there is no prescription for what should leave her lips. Or, she can be silent. While it certainly can be fun, talk isn't so important for men.

Again, avoid any lingering resentments, unfinished arguments, or concerns about housework. This is not the time. Give him a treat. And she should know this: Her man will now go into the world, perhaps appreciating, perhaps noticing, but certainly not *in need* of other women. He has his own woman and this is all he needs. She has brilliantly and skillfully made up for any inequity of erotic desire. Not only is he more apt to be loyal, but he will also be happier, more peaceful, kinder, and - it has already been proven - healthier, physically and psychologically. This is a woman's simple defense against infidelity - physical and visual - and for the problem of a man who, in the vicinity of a beautiful woman, has not learned the subtle art of discretion.

While the knowledge of loving a woman seems endless and stretches the male intellect in ways he may never have considered, the techniques needed for pleasing a man are quite simple. But this is a male point of view. It may seem infinitely complex to women. She may wonder: Why *does* he want sex so often? Or, if he looks at another woman, it's *not* a breach of our sacred bond? How can this be?

In other words, we need to have patience with our own ignorance, and with the ignorance of our partners.

Men need to learn that a real man - *and* a great lover - is not determined by the size of his genitals (an idea perpetrated by male enhancement ads) or the number of women he's had sex with. It is rather, a question of whether he can understand the needs of his partner and learn to truly please her. An infidelity does not imply greater virility, but rather, that something is amiss in the primary relationship. Consider the man who says, "My wife is no great shakes in bed," then runs off to another woman. Of course, there's an undeniable thrill in exploring, Lewis and Clark style, the body of another person, but he should first try to become a more adept lover at home. When he does, not only will the quality and quantity of sex increase, but also sheer pride in his expertise - his competence - will fill the vacuum that might send him afield.

And why be sub-par with two lovers?

Please one like a wizard. It will be enough.

And a woman should also take pride in her expertise. She is keeping her man happy. In knowing exactly what to do, she feels more womanly.

J   J   J

My own thoughts, as I drained the last of a third pint, were on Maureen.

Was she, at this moment, opening that one magical drawer, whose contents celebrate the luscious mystery of femininity? A drawer filled with enticing lacy garments that inspire thrilling French words such as *décolletage*? Was she swimming a hand through a sea of silk and wondering: *I wonder why James is coming over tonight*?

"Let me see if I understand this," I said. "Women create this whole charade of non-responsibility... so they didn't *choose* to go to bed with you; they simply *ended up* there. So when the day of reckoning comes-"

"Something like that."

"Well, fine," I said. "Blame me. Make love to me, but blame me. Then send me to Hell. I'll go happily."

I thought: *Just kidding, God.* Then I said, "And what if she accuses me of seducing her?"

"Don't worry about it," Tony said.

"Why?" I said. "Why shouldn't I worry about it? I hate to be accused when I haven't-"

"I know. Everyone does. Just know why she's doing it."

"And why is she-"

"Because she's hurt. She's given you her most precious gift and you didn't seem to appreciate it. She puts the blame on you to ease her pain," he said. "Seduction is a myth. No one goes unwillingly. But this won't be a problem, my friend. From this moment forward, you will always appreciate it. She will never feel hurt."

Now I was truly in a quagmire. If I sleep with Maureen, what *is* she expecting? Of course she knows I'm married. Will that mean anything to her?

I thought for a moment, and then looked up at Tony. "So, you just said 'why be sub-par with two lovers?' What about, say, hypothetically, pleasing two like a wizard? Anything wrong with-"

"You mean if no one finds out? Only this: The 'other woman' will probably expect more. A woman who gives you her precious gift assumes you have plans to leave your primary relationship and make a commitment with her. For most women, it's an unspoken agreement. In making love to her, in her mind, you have willingly signed on the dotted line. There are exceptions, but for the most part, women just don't do casual sex. Nor do they understand it. After that first, impetuous tumble, in all likelihood, it's nothing but problems. '*Why didn't you call me? Did you tell your wife about us yet? When are you going to tell her? You're not going to tell her? Why did you make love to me in the first place?*' She will ask questions that make absolutely no sense to you! But any honest answer leaves you sounding like some kind of immoral rodent. How *will* you answer? That lust is constant and oppressive and she *was simply available*? Can you imagine the look on her face?"

"But what *is* the answer?" I said. "I mean, sometimes... you know, sometimes you're tearing your hair out with lust. Your skin is crawling with ten species of vermin, your joints ache, your teeth ache, every woman you see drives you beyond insanity, and a woman - a woman is suddenly flirting her gorgeous ass off with you - and you make, what I guess is politely called *an overture*. I mean, you're ready to shove hot butter knives through your skull, ready to commit mass - *stop grinning!*"

"You're getting ahead of me," Tony said, grinning.

So, Maureen. Flirty Maureen. I always thought the flirtatious ones were the least promiscuous, but you never knew. Maybe she's one of the few women who understand casual sex. Maybe she's easy about it. *Easy.* But then, Jesus, who even knows where she's been? She's certainly no novice at attracting men. Maybe I should grab some condoms on the way.

Condoms.

If Cindy finds out about all of this - and this is small town - could I say with a contrite voice, "It just happened. It just sort of... there we were." Then, of course she'll ask if I used a condom. I know her. And what do I say then? Yes, I did. And she will say, "So you went to her house, and bought condoms on the way?" After a moment, I'll see the trap I have stupidly fallen into. She'll consider my answer for a moment. Then, realization will strike. "You bought condoms on the way, and you tell me it 'just happened?'" I'll feel as bad for being trapped as I will for my transgression.

Okay.

I could go to Maureen's *without* condoms. I could let fate take its mindless course, *not* use a condom, and be able to claim semi-non-culpability. Gripped unwillingly in the throes of lust. If she finds out, well, one thing simply led to another. Which will of course divert the discussion to the drought of passion in our own marriage, and perhaps shine the ugly light of blame upon her. This diversion will hold me for one minute, if that. She will then bring back the simple, cold fact, that not only have I cheated, not only have I broken the sacred bond of our marriage, but now, we *both* might have AIDS, and how could I risk *both* of our lives. We have two children, she will remind me.

The moral high ground will be hers any way I turn.

I could get her a copy of Kundera's book, and highlight the part where it says; *this has nothing to do with my wife.* I could add that it was nothing more than... breakfast with a friend. But she won't understand this in the slightest.

I could tell her, "Cindy. Your thinking is sadly limited by your tragically myopic gender-centricity. A common, yet forgivable pitfall among women. If you could just open your mind a tad-"

Who in hell am I kidding?

Jesus, don't people do this stuff all the time? Do they get this neurotic? I don't want to be neurotic now; I want to feel confident and sexy. And suave. Am I serious? I think I am. Men do this. We do it and it's just a matter of secrecy. Of covering our tracks.

Jesus, I sound like a criminal.

Still... Maureen. I bet she's sorting through her lingerie at this very moment, which, I imagine, looks pretty amazing on her. Oh, dear God in heaven. The very scent of her! What is that scent? Something French, no doubt. Everything erotic is French.

Would there really be a horrendous breach?

"Are all women like that?" I asked, "Unable to have casual sex?"

"No," he said, "Some can. We had a sexual revolution in the sixties and seventies. Lots of women were having casual sex with a lot of different men. But now, these women are in their 50's and 60's, and are reporting that the sexual revolution was a scam for women - it didn't meet their needs at all - while it was hog heaven for men. A similar kind of casual sex fad occurs today among young people called 'hooking up'. I don't know much about it, but I'm guessing women will remember it with same sort of distasteful nostalgia twenty years from now. Once a woman understands and accepts the time, patience, and emotional connection she truly needs in intimacy, when she knows what good lovemaking is really about - which I would guess the young women involved in hooking up don't understand quite yet - then she has a barometer for comparison. A true understanding and acceptance of her needs may take many years. Some women can be casual, but most can't. They try it out and it doesn't work for them."

I wondered: was Maureen among that small percentage that can be casual?

Who knows? How could I possibly know? I only knew one thing. Tonight, if I do go through with this, I want to dazzle. Do it right or don't do it at all. Light up the damn firmament.

"Tony," I said. "Is there more?"

"There's more," he said. "Do you know about the g-spot?"

"The G spot?" I said. "Does it really-"

T   T   T

It exists.

We can either let it baffle us and ignore it, or we can thank our creator for yet another way to make the women we love moan with delight and love us all the more. Real men - competent men - know about the g-spot. While it's nice if we can tune up her car, this will only get us a polite thank you. A moan of delight is infinitely more gratifying.

The Enlightened Hand

Future historians will certainly look back on the present as the Sexual Dark Ages. Imagine the disbelief on the face of a beautiful,

24th century co-ed, the eraser of her pencil pressed quizzically against her lovely, dimpled cheek as she asks her professor, "You mean... they didn't even *know* about the g-spot until the late 20th century?"

The learned prof will nod his head sadly but sagely. "The G, the Y, and even spot B-38!"

The students will gasp in astonishment.

"But the G spot!" He will say, lighting his pipe. "Even then - even when they knew about it - it was ignored or shrouded in mystery." He will then pause dramatically, gaze off in a moment of scholarly reflection and add, "I'm afraid those were frightfully barbaric times."

Do we really wish to be remembered as barbarians?

Attende: The g-spot is located just inside the upper part of the vagina, behind the pubic bone. It feels nubbly, like a cat's tongue. Whenever you touch a vagina, always make sure your hands are clean and your nails are manicured. Again, don't touch her here until she's hot, wet, and ready. But when she is - with one or two fingers, depending upon what she's comfortable with - touch this place, press gently upwards and pull back toward the opening. Try different pressures and speeds, but super slow works quite well. See how she responds. A g-spot seems to be more sensitive when she is warmed up rather than during preliminary touching. We can't know how a g-spot or a clitoris feels, so pay attention to her response. Or simply ask, though she may be too shy to tell you. Listen to her breathing, etc.

A g-spot and a clitoris can easily be touched at the same time. Place an index finger – or two fingers, depending on the size of her opening - inside the vagina on the g-spot. Place a thumb on the clitoris. Pull out and up on the g-spot and touch lightly on the clitoris, moving slowly. The hand is C-shaped, almost like a pinching motion – but lightly on the clitoris - with one or two fingers around the pubic bone, on her g- spot. But it's so natural that a hand should be here, in this very configuration, that you would wonder if our creators designed a hand for just this purpose. Experiment with pressures and motions. But it's best to keep the motion slow and steady, moving your hand in and out, pressing upwards against the g-spot on the pull out. Ask her how it feels. (If she tells you to just shut up and keep going, consider this a compliment.)

For this next method, your hand must be absolutely clean. From the C-shape (palm up) position, turn your hand slightly, so your palm faces her inner thigh, and simply add the knuckle of your middle or (ringless) ring finger, pressing it against her anus - a very erotic area. As you move your hand in and out or gently twisting, stimulating all three very exciting areas. You might ask her: faster? Slower? Harder? Easier?

Above all, keep your knuckle - the one on her anus - away from her vagina. (It's probably best to try this after she's taken a bath or shower.) Again, if she's not very wet, use a little lubricant.

A slight variation on the clitoral swirls

Regarding the technique mentioned earlier - light, slow circles over the clitoris; here is delectable variation: Do this while gently kissing her mouth. As if women aren't baffling enough! As we mentioned, a fabulous connection exists between the mouth and the clitoris. To stimulate both of these at once, well, as one woman said, "It makes you crazy!" Rubbing her nipples back and forth are also wonderful ways to augment touching her down below.

Also, regarding the light, slow circles over the clitoris, if this doesn't seem to have much effect, try a light, upward, flicking motion. This might just send her over the edge. Above all, because every woman is different, it's quite important to ask her what feels good, and to experiment. Make her your erotic project. Study her. Take a problem-solver's interest in this sweet bit of wonder beside you as you unlock her fabulous, challenging mysteries. It may take a few sessions to know what works.

Still, it's easy to err on the side of being too rough. Keep your fingers wet - use lubricant if necessary - and always remember: go slow, be gentle.

Here's something else worth a try. My girlfriend liked it so much she began shouting, "Yes! Yes! Yes! Yes!" The technique, since then, has been called, "Yes-yes," but feel free to adopt any name that strikes you. It goes like this. With wet fingers, gently hold (lightly pinch) her clitoris, from the sides, between your thumb and forefinger. Pull it very gently away from her body. Lightly roll it between your fingers. If she says, "Oh my!" well, you have your name. It's good to name things: a private, secret code between you and your lover. Some luscious technique from your prodigious inventory of skills can be requested on demand. The goofier the name, the better.

The Plunge, is another fabulous technique that every man should have in his repertoire. Of course, she needs to be wet. If she isn't wet enough, put a little lubricant on her and your fingertips.

You have already mastered the light, slow touching of the clitoris as explained earlier. Touch her clitoris with your two middle fingers. Move lightly, gently, slowly, up one side, down the other. Also, move on either side of it, gliding it between your two fingers. Also, go up and down the labias. Include them, but focus on the clitoris. Lightly, slowly. Continue until she's hot, wet, and ready. You can determine this by her breathing, and how she moves. As a woman gets aroused, her hips may begin to jerk spasmodically, or she might move toward your fingers, in anticipation of your touch.

Then slide your two middle fingers into her vagina. Upon entry, curl them up and under the pubic bone, gracing the g-spot. Then back out, up and over the clitoris. Circle the clitoris lightly, slowly, maybe three or four times. Then dip your two fingers back inside again. Add lubricant if necessary. (If a woman doesn't get very wet, always use lubricant when touching her vagina. If she's dry, she can easily get worn out, raw, and require recovery time. Lubricant ensures plenty of frequent sex.) Depending upon the size of her opening, you may wish to use only one finger. If two fingers work - say if she's had a child - use two fingers. Why? *A vagina needs to be gently stretched.* This replicates the pleasure of penetration and for many women is just as satisfying as intercourse. For women who require penetration, the plunge not only replicates it wonderfully, but also

James Cahill

may even do a better job of stimulating the entire vagina. She may gasp with pleasure at your first plunge. Again, don't dip in too soon; wait until she's very wet and very ready. And then, she will probably continue to moan with each subsequent plunge. Again, three or four light, slow circles around the clitoris, then, slowly, plunge inside. Pull out slowly, sliding your fingertips against the g-spot, then lightly move them around the clitoris a few times. Then plunge again. You needn't go too far inside. Up to your second knuckle is fine, but you might experiment by going farther. Maintain a slow rhythm. Do not feel a need to speed up. Speed is always a mistake down here. As an experiment, try going *very* slowly. Focus on a very... slow... pull out... gliding... your fingertips... over the g-spot. Women seem to feel more on the pull out then the push in, and slowness here gives her an excruciating sense of pleasure. When she is about to come, you might push your fingers a bit deeper into her vagina.

Simultaneous kissing is great, and so is sucking on a breast, or rubbing her nipple with a finger. The combination of the plunge with breast stimulation will drive your woman crazy. Sucking a breast is easiest. To use your hand, if you lay on her left side, it's easiest to go for her right breast. Your left hand touches her vagina. Place your right elbow along your ribs, and reach for the closest, her left breast. Try pressing upward with the side of your index finger to sort of prop it up, and rub her nipple - back and forth slowly - with your thumb. While a breast can be rubbed a bit harder, a good pace is about one second in each direction. Back... and forth... back... and forth. Or, as stated earlier, cup her breast in your hand and gently massage it, one then the other.

Keep everything slow, steady. Talk, or let her drift in her thoughts, her fantasies. If you feel her getting dry down below, have a squeeze bottle of lubricant ready. She can also place a few drops on herself if she feels like she needs it. Again, don't rush toward a goal, just continue to touch her down below, kiss her, or suck or touch one of her breasts. And know that she is basking in pure pleasure. Do not speed up or touch her harder in order to make it build. It will build on its own. Just proceed slowly, gently and steadily - and let her fall into an orgasm.

Nice combinations

Another technique that works quite well is a one or two fingers on her g-spot with a clitoral kiss. With your mouth, suck gently on her clitoris. This is best managed from the side, so the two of you are perpendicular. As she lies on the bed, kneel beside her. Or, stand beside the bed, and have her put one leg over your shoulder. Again, begin with the preliminaries; kissing, touch her gently all over, get her hot, get her wet. Don't touch her down below with your hand until she's wet. (The knuckle on the tush is optional. Try it and see how she responds. Some women love this, some may not. If not, just using one or two fingers on the g-spot is quite effective.) As you touch her, gently lick or suck on her clitoris - not hard; just play with it gently and slowly with your tongue. As she gets hotter and wetter, even if she begins to moan, again, do not go faster or harder. That's not how women operate. *A continued, slow, gentle, dependable rhythm is what women love.* This is what enables her to get lost in your touch. (If you stop or shift to another speed, the flow and consequent ability to get lost is disrupted.) Keep up the same, gentle action with your fingers - in and out, on the g-spot - as described above, the slower the better. Don't force her. Again, let her fall into an orgasm.

Experiment with clitoral swirls, the plunge, the C-shaped hand, or using your mouth and hand simultaneously – one or more techniques will usually be successful. And of course, these techniques are to be used after a good warm-up of slow, gentle, focused touching, on her less erotic areas.

Very important: When a woman has an orgasm through skilled use of your hand, particularly with your fingers inside of her, you can feel it. She may arch up her hips, but always, you will feel a sudden, spasmodic tightening and quivering around your fingers. This is difficult to feel with a penis but easy to feel with fingers. So there can be no fakery, no need to look for the 'post-orgasmic flush' (a redness in the chest area) as proof that you've successfully pleasured your woman. No need to ask, no need for her to fake one. You have all the proof, in that miraculous quivering, that you have not only pleasured her, but that you are a fabulous lover.

Your woman can count on you for an orgasm, and this can create a sea change in a relationship. Intimacy is no longer an event full of angst, rancor, asking, cajoling, or of one person doing a grudging favor for another. It is, instead, a secret and wonderful event that you both happily anticipate and share - the miracle of an orgasm, and the physical and spiritual peace that follows.

And because you have been mindful of keeping her lubricated, you can have sex even later that same day if you desire, because there has been absolutely no wear and tear on that delicate part of her. As we said before, with typical intercourse, most women report that 2-4 bouts of lovemaking a week is their absolute max. That number, my friends, is out the window. A) Because you now have many more effective alternatives to intercourse. B) Because she has been kept lubricated and experiences no pain. And most important - C) because she has had an orgasm.

These three simple facts will make her want sex more often, maybe as much as her man wants it. Once a woman knows that something amazing is guaranteed, she will become a willing and avid lover. Even if she is still too shy to initiate, she will certainly respond positively when he reaches for her amorously, and she feels his slow and gentle touch on her body.

When using hands to make love, take turns. The notion of the simultaneous orgasm as the pinnacle of sexual pleasure is a myth. To pleasure your partner while your partner is trying to pleasure you is distracting and can frustrate both efforts. When you please your woman, let her bask and languish in your skillful touch. Then, relax, lie back, and let her pleasure you.

It's not variety of positions that make for sex great. The key is to know what works. An orgasm is never boring. Once a man understands how everything works down there, he can certainly invent his own methods if he likes and if he sees that his lover enjoys them. And remember, your woman will want to be held afterwards. A woman who has had an orgasm and is held afterwards will be happy to please you and be pleased by you again and again.

Your lover will never again see sex as a burden or an obligation. Imagine, giving her that certain look during dinner, and she smiles and her eyebrows dance with anticipation. Because you've proven yourself a worthy lover, the foreplay has in fact, already begun, and you have created a wonderfully willing partner. My girlfriend and I, who frequently used our hands in lovemaking, found that these methods brought sex out of the mysterious realm, into a lighter place where we discussed it easily and enjoyed it regularly. She often said, "Let's make love *before* we go out, so we can just relax and watch people." We would pleasure each other, and then off we would go, floating into the night on a magic carpet of post-orgasmic bliss.

The orgasm!

Can anyone sing its praises enough? A mood enhancer, stress reliever, and before bed, a wonderful sleep aid. (For the man who complains that women like to talk after sex: Gentlemen. Give her an orgasm and she'll go right to sleep.)

To the uninitiated, use of hands may be considered a mere appetizer, or an activity for junior high kids but not for adults. But using hands for lovemaking can be wonderful as a main course. Consider: a guaranteed female orgasm – as opposed to a less than 30% occurrence with intercourse - and no worries over pregnancy or performance. It is almost completely safe regarding STI's, though herpes can be transferred via breaks in the skin. A woman named Alison told me she considered intercourse a major production, with all of the prepping for protection, and thus, she and her husband rarely had sex. Using hands is simple, casual, accessible, and worry free. And a free mind allows a couple to lose themselves in lovemaking more completely. Also, with intercourse, men may feel tremendous pressure – both to not come too soon and to not lose their erection. Staying in this excited-but-not-too-excited middle ground can be challenging. When lovemaking is so effortful, it becomes difficult to relax, to enjoy the experience, and to have those wonderful orgasms that can only happen when one surrenders completely to a partner. (And a hand will never explode and go limp.)

'Surrender' in sex is a fascinating concept. Many women, commendably, find their way to a climax with an unskilled lover by simply taking responsibility for their own orgasm. Here, a man only needs to last long enough. But to surrender to a lover – to relinquish control over what is most vulnerable, and to climax through a partner's skillful abilities - is far more exciting.

If penetration is on the agenda, try giving her one or more orgasms with your hand and/or mouth first, and then have intercourse. These techniques are excellent as effective foreplay.

How a man brings his woman to an orgasm is up to the couple, and, with an eye for what works for a particular woman. All women are different. It may take awhile for a woman to become receptive to use of hands, and many women simply prefer the feel of penetration. Just be mindful of the risks and be responsible.

Communication

Every woman is a puzzle.

Experimentation is necessary; and men and women need to speak openly about what works and what doesn't. Because a man has no vagina, no female body or brain, he has no way of knowing how his touch feels to a woman. He can try these techniques, and his woman may respond: 'that's great,' 'that's wonderful,' or, 'be gentle'. Expect to hear "be gentle" and "go slow" often, as the light, slow touch is the most difficult for men to understand. Even as a man's touch improves exponentially, he will still hear these two suggestions: go slow... be gentle.

Respond: "Okay." or "Thank you."

In the past, as I mentioned before, in my dark days as a pathetic lover, any suggestion from a woman struck as a direct hit to my sense of competence. Often I was hurt and angry. Women have told me: men are so sensitive! Even the kindliest suggestion can be received as criticism, and a touchy individual may respond with exasperation. Now, I hear suggestions differently. Because I have no way of knowing how my touch feels to her, I can only gauge by her physical reactions and by what she tells me. So I'm grateful. Anything she tells me is an opportunity for me to be a better lover, and, in fact, to be more competent as a man.

When inept lovemaking occurs among partners who are reluctant to communicate, nothing will change and the classic standoff may result: the woman will fend off the man's overtures, lovemaking will be infrequent, and she may fake an orgasm to end a painful situation quickly.

What can undermine communication?

As we've said, an overly sensitive partner may misinterpret suggestions as a critique, and respond in anger. Sometimes, the communication actually *is* unkind. Unkindness is often predicated with a false assumption that everyone should already know what to do - when we don't - and thus talking is unnecessary. The woman who requires the illusion of being 'swept away' may find that making specific requests to her man is particularly vexing to the fantasy. Suffice to say, an unkind comment can severely undermine follow-up attempts at intimacy.

And many couples make love in silence simply out of shyness.

If your woman is silent, and you ask how something feels, she may say, "Everything you do is wonderful," which is a lie, but much easier than honesty. If a woman's language is vague, ask her to be specific, or let her guide your fingers to show you what she wants. Still, she may not know. She may not know she even has a right to ask you to meet her needs.

Try to draw her out, but if she really has a difficult time talking about sex, take a step-by-step approach. You might ask, "How does this feel? This?"

She may still be too shy to respond. If this is the case, attend to her heartbeat, her breathing, the movement of her body, her hips, etc. With time, she might begin to communicate more. Don't give up on a woman who won't talk about sex. People, for the most part, are afraid to discuss it. In fact, it's easier to have sex than to talk about it. For some women, talking about sex indicates a kind of loose, unwholesomeness they want to avoid.

As communication improves, try your best to gently encourage your partner to be as specific as possible. Try to move beyond vague standbys, like "Take time," and "Everything you do is wonderful." Still, consider a few of the women you know and imagine how many could, say, for example: "Take your index finger, dip it into the honey pot, then swirl it lightly over the clitoris."

James Cahill

Someday we may all chat with such clarity. But most of us can't, and thus, don't be surprised if, for the most part, you're on your own. So while communication is important, don't depend on her to help you figure her out. Learn the techniques outlined here. Try them. If one technique fails, try another. Attend to her body language, her breathing, her heartbeat, and any sounds she makes. Make her your erotic project.

It's also very important to listen. If she asks you to slowly touch her back, then by God, touch her back. Don't feel threatened, or feel a need to show her you know better as to how and where to touch her. Hold off on where you want to place your hand. She's giving you instructions on how to become the man she will want to make love to again and again, so give her exactly what she asks for.

Finally, it's very important to know what not to say. The West Africans have a proverb: Teasing is dangerous.

Avoid confusing lighthearted goofiness with teasing. Make no jokes about her body, her breast size, about what occurred in bed, or about anything that might be taken wrongly. When couples become intimate, everyone feels extremely exposed and vulnerable. It would be sexual suicide, for example, to imitate her passionate moaning with the mistaken idea that you are being playful. If she loves sex, don't call her a sex maniac. Don't call her a nympho. Such mistakes will destroy a partner's trust and consequent ability to surrender. It may take awhile to regain trust, to allow your partner, once again, to feel safe with you.

Again, lovers should make this agreement: all suggestions will be delivered politely. Each will be received with gratitude - a verbal 'thank you' - because they arrive as opportunities to make us better lovers. And most important: take nothing personally.

I strongly advise this to be a spoken agreement.

And sealed with a kiss.

Rancor will evaporate. Sex will become better and better as a man becomes very good at knowing what his lover wants. Remember, the body of the other gender is strange, alien territory. We cannot be blamed if we're not born with the knowledge of great lovers. If something goes amiss, forgive yourself; it's part of the learning process. Then try something else.

Penetration, a word about condoms

If, however, you plan to have intercourse, and you wish to avoid pregnancy and STD's - if you're with a new partner - use a condom, or one of the gels or spermicides with nonoxynol-9.

An early complaint regarding condoms - always from women - was that they 'spoil the spontaneity of love making'. Translated: with all the discussion, getting up to get them, unwrapping, fiddling, unrolling, there was a moment for conscious, calculated planning, and thus, how could a woman claim afterwards to having been 'swept away' by passion?

What is the solution for a good number for men?

They choose not to use a condom.

Condoms - using them, buying them, discussing them – can undermine the blithe, spontaneous moment. A condom forces a moment of deliberate action, which makes everyone morally culpable. The woman risks being called a bad girl, the man risks losing a golden opportunity. Unprotected sex can often be the result.

But this is changing. Though women are taking more responsibility - in asking men out, initiating sex, carrying condoms in purses - bad-girl guilt may be diminishing in some, but in others it may simply be an insurmountable aspect of being female. Regardless, have condoms ready; don't feel shy about using them. Of course, you can also avoid intercourse and do other things - like using your hands skillfully if you both desire. Of course, with intercourse, a man must proceed with an eye for what she will expect from him after he makes love to her. Consider this before it gets ugly later. And know that you have plenty of options. If an enlightened hand can do more than a penis, it certainly makes sense to avoid the problems of STD's, pregnancy, the dulling effects of condoms, and the differing notions as to what your lovemaking meant. You can avoid many problems just by simply using your hands. But, if intercourse is where you're headed, with all the problems it can involve, it

James Cahill

is certainly important to cut through the silence and remember that safe sex is everyone's responsibility.

Trust, Surrender, the very last comment on affairs, and A Few Other Absolutely Wonderful Ideas.

You've touched her slowly and gently; touched her secret, wonderfully feminine places in the ways described or in ways you have discovered with your own breathtaking sense of invention, and she's wet and deliciously hot and you both wish to have safe intercourse.

Maybe a condom is already on and don't you look dapper.

Dashing, aerodynamic and rakish.

Maybe you're not using a condom and are taking other precautions.

Regardless, as a man of the world, you're in no hurry. Lust has no mastery over you. You will proceed at your own, supremely competent leisure. Perhaps you feel a bit naughty. Before you enter her, when she's wet - and this is great, with or without a condom - hold your penis and rub, up and down, over the opening of her vagina. Up and down, slowly. You're in no hurry and you could do this forever. She will soon - trust me - be in agony for you to enter her. What a surprising bit of irony: she, in agony for *you* to enter *her*! But why rush? In fact, why not have a little fun. Keep rubbing.

"Is now a good time?" you ask.

She'll nod anxiously. "Yes, it is."

Keep rubbing.

"How about now?" you ask.

She'll tell you it's a very good time.

"Are you sure?"

Keep rubbing.

"What about now?" you say.

Happily drive your woman to the brink of insanity. Torture her as long as you wish. And oh, her gratifying gasp when you finally enter her!

Notice a few of things here. You are in the driver's seat. You are not a powerless victim of rushing hysteria, a slave to your lust. You are taking your woman exactly where you wish to take her.

Patience underscores everything you do. Notice also: you can play with her anticipation. You don't enter her before she's ready. You don't even enter *when* she's ready. You wait until she's *excruciatingly* ready.

A woman who removes her clothes for you and opens her legs for you is a woman who surrenders to you. Again, if we understand the concept of surrender in a woman - which she expresses when she snuggles up kittenishly, or sits in your lap - we go a long way toward understanding what a woman needs. She needs to feel safe and cared for. She desperately needs to be able to trust you, and a woman's trust is not a thing to be trifled with.

But when you have her trust, playing with her anticipation adds a spicy twist to the concept of surrender. She can't predict you. Engage the imp, who is playful and will hurt no one.

Nicole, a friend who is anything but shy, told me of a boy-friend who was a wonderful lover. Of course, I wanted to hear more. I wanted details; graphic, shocking details, and though her tendency for feminine euphemism was still in operation, she didn't disappoint.

"You know, I can't predict him," she told me, then said no more.

I asked what she meant.

She took a breath and exhaled, as if she knew I would push it - which I would - and she said, "You know, when you're, like, kissing your way up a woman's leg-"

I nodded my head, though I'm certain I'd never done such a thing.

"-and you get to her thigh, then to the top of her thigh, and then, you *skip* right to her stomach?"

I came clean. I admitted I had never attempted such a feat. I imagined her boyfriend's brazen, surprising leap: thigh to stomach. I asked, "And you liked that?"

"Mmmm...." she said, her voice suddenly dreamy. "It drives me crazy. Cause then, when he finally *does* kiss me there, it's like, *oh my God!*"

So, while a bit of fun with her anticipation is the point here, it's also true that there are supremely gifted lovers out there - male and female - and I wish they would all be identified and asked to give seminars. Everyone has some delectable bits to share. Why keep them secrets? Who wouldn't want to learn such things?

Here is another way to drive your woman to ecstasy.

When you are inside of her - in the missionary position - all the way inside, notice a wonderful little quirk of God's creation. Your pubic bone is right up against her clitoris. What a stunningly perfect arrangement!

Proof that God exists and loves us?

Consider this, but fleetingly. Plenty of time later for cosmological questions.

As you move, blissfully in and out – again, a slow, steady rhythm works best - try moving your pubic bone against her clitoris. Another variation is to try angling your penis at a downward angle to rub her clitoris as you move in and out.

Something, by now, should bring her to a climax. You've touched her slowly and gently. You've spoken to her. Perhaps you've had intercourse. If this doesn't bring her to breakthrough, don't worry. Some women have a very difficult time achieving an orgasm. This may be a problem of trust. If a woman has been with selfish, uncaring, unkind or unskilled lovers, she may take awhile to trust you before she can surrender to the point of actually having an orgasm. Give her time and patience. Earn her trust. It also may take some time to discover what brings her to an orgasm. But finally, an orgasm is not the barometer of success. The care and attention you've given her is. A woman will often comment that you took time, and how much she loved it. And men who take time are quite rare. Still, odds of her having an orgasm will be infinitely better - if not, guaranteed - when the man knows what his lover needs.

Try other positions. She can be on top, where she has more control of her movements. Or, you can enter her from behind while she kneels or lies on her stomach. This is a good way to stimulate the g-spot during intercourse. Or she can lay on her side with one knee up toward her chest while he enters her from the back.

For some men, condoms are difficult to climax with. For such men, a woman can reach around and massage his balls. This may be successful.

As you lay on top of her in the missionary position, she can place her legs together, with your legs around and outside of hers. This will grab you sweetly but firmly inside of her. With or without a condom, for a man, this is sheer delight. You will probably detonate happily. If, during sex, for some reason you feel yourself losing your erection, this technique will perk you right up. Because it's so exciting for the man, use it only when you're ready to come or if you need a brief recharge.

Bear in mind, condoms slip off. If she's not wet, they can break. Check periodically to make sure it's still on and unbroken. The leg-together technique can cause condoms to come off, so be particularly careful when using it. Dryness can make a condom slip off, break, or cause irritation to the woman. If she has a tendency to get dry, use a lubricant.

Don't feel shy about purchasing any of these. Condoms, lubricants, birth-control gels – just look the cashier in the eye and dare them to crack a joke. They won't anyway. After the first purchase, it's easy. Plunk your money down; look bored.

Lack of lubrication in a woman can be a crisis of confidence. She might feel something is wrong with her. Anything can cause it; a salty meal like a pepperoni pizza, or simple nervousness. If you need a lubricant, use one. It's a small detail, and with the right attitude, it too, can be plenty of fun.

If, because of the condom, you can't come inside of her, exit and let her rub you with her hand.

You have made love. You are in no danger of pregnancy, HIV, or any other sexually transmitted disease. In addition, with effective touching and more frequent sex as a consequence, both partners are satisfied. Two satisfied partners are apt to be monogamous.

A quick word about oral sex.

When I worked on a fishing boat in Alaska, because the fishing industry employs men almost exclusively, the talk was frequently about women and sex. Something obnoxious and wonderful occurs among men when women are not around. The chatter is graphic, crude, and for the man who grew up feeling timid around earthier topics, oddly liberating. The boat I worked on employed a skipper and two sixteen-year-old boys. Though I knew things had changed since I was a young man, I was still somewhat shocked when both boys claimed to have experienced giving oral sex to a woman. I asked if they had any advice. The question was partly tongue in cheek, as I sort of hoped they would ask me for advice. But teenagers, almost by definition, know everything and the taller of them spoke. "Go for the nub-nub." he said.

Of course, we roared with laughter.

Fish, talk about sex, laugh. This seemed the rhythm of the fisherman. I believe I heard every pussy joke ever conceived during my stint on a fishing boat in Alaska. I was truly surprised to hear a few such jokes told by women.

But their advice was surprisingly on the money. So, build up the suspense. Kiss her leg, her inner thigh, and her stomach. Then, touch your tongue lightly to her outer lips, and her inner lips. Then, gently, move your tongue back and forth over the clitoris, just as you did with your finger.

The other bit of counsel the young man offered was equally noteworthy: "Don't try to do with your tongue what a penis does."

He didn't use the word penis (probably no one in Alaska does) but he was correct here too. Don't try to enter her in this way. Lick her clitoris, gently. Again, as she gets hotter, there is no need to be rougher or harder. Simply move your tongue over the clitoris, gently, lightly, slowly, as if you have all the time in the world. Help her 'fall' into an orgasm. And, as mentioned before, women seem to love it if you place a finger or two inside of her and gently rub her g-spot.

One woman, Julia, gave me some excellent advice that had never occurred to me. We were quietly talking about this wonderful act in an elegant Italian restaurant - actually, the perfect place for such a discussion.

"You know," she said. "There's more to it."

"What's that?" I asked.

She leaned across the table and whispered quietly, "You can suck."

We touched on this briefly earlier and it's good advice, I discovered. Very gently suck her clitoris, her labias, play with them lightly with your tongue.

And I thought about this, and other, lovely bits of advice. They always seem whispered, so secretly, so conspiratorially, and in truth, so rarely. I imagine a man or woman out there in the world who has stumbled upon some neuron shattering method that causes both partners to detonate so profoundly as to scatter their atoms across sixteen dimensions then snap back to corporal form leaving them in a coma for six weeks and a state of happy amnesia for twelve. I'm certain it exists, and we search for it like a method for turning metal into gold, like a lone philosopher looking for one honest man, and once we discover it, we'll say, "It's obvious! I should have thought of this long ago!"

But now, you've satisfied her to the best of your abilities.

And, it can't be emphasized too much, so we'll say it again: Hold her. Linger with her. Do it whether you're in the mood or not. Women need it and love it. After lovemaking women are most vulnerable. Horrible is the man who gets up for a beer or heads back to the ball game, or rolls over and falls asleep at this very crucial moment. Give her time. Talk to her. Be sweet. Be silly. Be a princely dallier, before and after you make love.

The miracle of women.

So, men are less emotionally connected to sex than women. Women see sex as a precious gift. Men can easily be casual about sex; women can't. This is the difference; neither is to blame. Men and women, for the most part, are meant to be together, but each brings to the pairing a desire that seems incongruous and often antagonistic to the other.

Dr. Carol Cassell, author of Swept Away, had a very interesting answer to the problem of this tension, and coming from a woman, it seemed somewhat surprising. She felt that women needed to think more like men. Meaning, women should be more cavalier about sex, less wrapped up in the 'precious gift' notion, and be able, if they wished, to have sex indiscriminately, like men. I was happy she did not deride males or accuse them of animal-like behavior. Mercifully, she uttered not a word of malice toward men. Women, she felt, should make the adjustment. A shocking, refreshing notion to hear from a woman.

I can see the logic in asking women to try to think more like men, to try to be less connected to sex emotionally. But women are women. For the most part lovemaking for a woman is an emotional experience. I don't believe it's possible for women to become more like men.

Can men become more like women? More emotional about sex? Less interested in other partners?

No, not really.

Rather than try to change women or men, wouldn't it be better if a man could recognize and appreciate the gift, with his voice, his touch, his patience?

A woman gives and she gives.

In *her* mind at least. To the male mind, lovemaking is an event we share with equity. Thus, when a woman *feels* like she's giving when she makes love, men don't, naturally, feel gratitude. Nor do we understand why she sees herself as giving in the first place. But, again, we don't know what it's like to have a vagina. The fact is this: if she thinks she's giving, *she is*. And of course, she expects to see us appreciating. Men must learn what is in a woman's mind and respect it. This is the first step in making the leap across the abyss. When we shift our behavior in bed - with a patient touch, a soothing voice - we begin to understand how women think, and ultimately, what the whole enterprise of lovemaking can be about.

The giving will then become reciprocal. Two lovers, reciprocating with generosity is a thrilling and lofty prospect. And so antithetical to the image created when a man speaks of 'getting some'. In truth, the man who thinks of lovemaking as 'getting some', probably, through no fault of his own, is getting very little. But one who truly knows how to give to a woman does not go against the grain of his male instinct. Rather, he enhances his instinct, and raises its possibilities to a higher level. To give to a woman is not agony, not a strain. In fact, it feels right and natural.

What seemed like tension becomes harmony.

On a continuum from vulgar to sublime, men - in general - tend more toward the vulgar end than women. And perhaps we are a vulgar rabble without women.

Women truly are our goddesses. Sublime. Exalted. Heavenly. They can lend dignity, elegance, and decorum to our lives. I love the way my own woman snuggles up, kittenishly with me on the couch. I love the way she likes to hold my hand, the way our feet touch under a table at a restaurant. A man's world is vastly different when he lives with a woman. He eats at the table. A napkin is folded under a fork and knife. His life feels cleaner, more orderly. The strong emotional aspect women feel in lovemaking elevates the event to a loftier place, and it's a place that a man, if he cares, will strive to reach and create for her. And his very life is uplifted.

His world is a scruffy place, otherwise. Women make it special.

If women become as unemotional as men about sex, lovemaking will lose it's elevated possibilities. Far better if we try our best to understand and accept the miracle of women; particularly the way they think and the way they struggle. If sex is a more emotional experience for her, of course she'll feel slighted if a man doesn't try to meet her in this more exalted realm. I marvel at how my thoughts can be filled with the erotic aspects of women, and, for so long, how little I understood the emotional depth and vulnerability of the woman connected to them. Certainly, the adolescent, thumbing his feverish way through a Playboy or clicking through adult websites does not understand this. This lack of understanding makes men swift, inept lovers. Once a man understands the whole woman rather than simply focusing on her sexual attributes - a focus seemingly programmed into him - lovemaking will not only improve, but will become much more frequent, and infinitely more satisfying for both partners.

And the days of begging and cajoling will be over. Not only will she respond positively to his sexual overtures, but she may also begin to initiate sex. She may take your hand and lead you to the bedroom. She may call and say, "I need to see you. I miss your touch." Your lovemaking will increase exponentially. And bear in mind this very real notion of the divine female – in Zorba the Greek, in the Da Vinci Code, etc., - recognized by many writers and thinkers, suggesting that with an understanding and reverence for the feminine, a kind of magic can occur that truly connects us with the sacred and miraculous. An attitude of 'getting some' won't get us there. But if our approach to intimacy is slow, caring, gentle and focused, we are soon filled, surrounded, and humming with something that might very well be called heaven. (And happily, without the tedious inconvenience of death.)

And while men should rise up to the loftier realm of women, women, for their part, should have compassion for the fact that men are hammered endlessly and mercilessly by a lust that is constant, oppressive, and for the most part, unconnected to emotion.

J   J   J

The place was nearly empty. The woman grinning into her salad left ages ago, certainly with a good tale for her best friend. Our little wonder of a waitress, along with the bartender, was watching us from the cash register, politely ready and waiting whenever we made a move that looked like an exit, to bring the bill.

It wasn't too late. Half past ten.

"So, what do you think?" Tony said after we had paid.

"You mean, will I write it?"

He nodded.

I hesitated. "You know, Tony, it's all thought-provoking stuff. And I must admit, I'm interested. Let's say all of these things work, that I road test your ideas and experience the fabulous success you suggest. That alone would benefit my life - my God - and every heterosexual man I know. More sex, better sex, feeling like a man who can please his woman! I mean, I need to try all of this out before I feel the excitement necessary to even think about writing a book. Jesus! What am I saying? *Write a book?*"

"I know," Tony said, "It's quite a-"

"It's a hell of a request," I said, "You're asking a lot here. I mean, wow; a book is a monster. To take on a project - such a big mother of a project; well, as I said, I'll road test it. See if I can find some resonance. If things turn out to be as exciting as you say, if I can find my own connection-"

He held up his hand. He nodded. I think he even smiled. Why a smile? We divvied up the bill, said our good-byes and headed to our cars.

Would I write Tony's book?

Tony's book. There was the problem. Did I really say, *resonance?* At least I didn't add, *in my soul.* But I think I was clear. At the moment though, I had a more immediate problem.

What to do? What to do? I sat in my parked car and hesitated a minute before I called. One ring. Two.

"Hello?"

"Maureen."

"Jim?"

"Maureen. How are you? I'm sorry. It's late. God, it's late-"

"It's not so-"

"Well, for *me*, you know. I'm just, wow, I'm just buried tomorrow. These damn finals to prepare. And a stack of essays I just remembered I have to grade. Just clean slipped my mind. You know they give us too many sections to teach. Everyone complains. Hey! Why am I telling you? You hear more whining than I do. I just didn't know things would take so- Christ, this friend of mine, God he can talk! He just goes on, you know? I lost track of time, and then, oh my God, I looked at my watch and damn near fell off my - hey, Momo. Momo, you there?"

"I'm here."

"Hey, forgive me, please? From the top of my head to the tip of my toes, I'm really, really - God, I feel so-" I released an exhale of

James Cahill

exasperation. "Listen. Maureen. Listen. Maybe next week," I said. "Can we take a rain check? Maybe next week?"

"Maybe next week," she said, slowly, always slowly. And in that slowness, I heard, painfully, the voice of a woman who knew the sound of a man who'd lost his nerve.

After a moment, I started the engine. I left.

It was late when I got home. The house was quiet. The porch light had a familiar, welcoming glow. The hall light too, was on. I stepped quietly down the hall, and gently pushed open the bedroom door. And there she lay. My Cindy. My wife. Bearer of my children. She had her back to me and was fast asleep. I sat on the bed, studied the rise of her hip, the smooth line of her thigh. I watched her slow and regular breathing.

I removed my clothes - every blessed stitch - and climbed in beside her. This woman. I had married her eight years ago. Here she was, as always. And as always, we did what we did, settling into a life, edging into a future... of what? My God, I've lived, not long, but long enough to know this: things can go nowhere. They can just sit there. Had I not done the best I could?

I traced my hand lightly, delicately along her shoulders, and then down the sweet declivity of her spine, and, to my own surprise, I was exploring this place for the first time in my life. She shivered. "Jim?"

"My goddess," I whispered.

End

Afterword:
For the socially conscious lover

Thousands of years ago, when far fewer of us walked the earth, humanity was encouraged to go forth and multiply. Then, it was excellent advice: our survival depended upon it. Today 7 billion crowd our planet, and 9.5 billion are predicted by the year 2050. The earth simply cannot support all of us. Population experts at Stanford concluded that the optimum number of people the earth can sustain is about 2 billion. That was the number in the early part of the 20th century. Of course, an accurate guess depends upon how much of everything each person uses, and certainly, we must learn to use the earth's precious gifts with equity, frugality, and an eye for the future. Bill Gates, who is currently putting much energy, brainpower, and money toward examining and solving world problems, has identified population reduction as a first priority. Reducing our carbon footprint can certainly be aided by reducing the number of feet making those prints.

Lovemaking vs. baby making.

The majority of pregnancies are unplanned.

If we wish to have children, few things work like intercourse. But when lust knocks with the frequency that it does, do we wish to risk producing a child every time we want to satisfy our passion? Unless a child is planned, how horrible are the words, "I missed my period," and the nightmarish decisions that can follow.

Lovers skilled in effective touching never need to worry about an accidental pregnancy. Though many cultural reasons may account for having many children (to care for parents in old age, a display of masculine prowess, and some religious sects promote unrestrained procreation) the need for intimacy, pleasure and a good old orgasm often results in intercourse and inadvertent procreation. When we know how to make love in other ways, we have children only when we choose to. The style of pleasuring that risks pregnancy is just one of many, and is often, far from the most satisfying for women. A first crucial step in slowing and reversing population growth might be to recast lovemaking and baby making as two distinct activities, and to enable anyone to avoid the risk of having an unplanned child, when all that's desired is to give and receive pleasure.

STI prevention

Anyone can learn these simple techniques for touching. Foams, gels, chemicals, pills, diaphragms, patches, and I.U.D.s - all of these can have harmful side effects. Chemicals can be toxic; they can burn, and condoms reduce sensitivity. (Nonoxynol - 9, a popular HIV preventer, can actually increase HIV transference, because it can damage the skin inside the vagina.) For effective touching, nothing more than a lubricant is needed if a woman's own lubrication is not enough. We are not meant to require a pharmacy in order to engage in the most basic and natural of human activities.

It is virtually impossible to contract HIV or any other sexually transmitted disease when hands are used to make love. (Shared needles are separate problem requiring a separate solution.) 'Virtually' because if one partner has a break in the skin herpes might be transferred. But skin does a fabulous job of protecting us from a host of deadly critters. (Hand washing is recommended before and after touching our partners.) No bodily fluids are shared. Currently, about 36 sexually transmitted diseases have been identified. 40-50% of people have herpes. Chlamydia is a bit higher. Odds are better than 50% that if we have unprotected intercourse with a new partner, we'll get something. Regarding STI's, with effective touching, we can make love virtually worry-free. Because most women cannot climax with intercourse, and because hands are much more effective, we will have a much greater possibility of giving our partner an orgasm.

Might this be an effective way to fight the AIDS pandemic?

Some believe that HIV is actually the earth's immune response to over population. If this is true, then effective touching, with it's natural pregnancy prevention, doesn't actually fight the virus. Rather, it works in collusion with nature to reduce the number of pregnancies. If bodily fluids are not shared an illness cannot be transmitted. In addition, when we successfully please a woman, we create a more willing partner, and a willing partner, as pointed out earlier, leads to monogamy. Monogamy is far and away, the most important factor in AIDS prevention.

Encouraging people to try other options to conventional sexual intercourse would be a huge challenge. It's difficult to change what is finally, very private behavior. But certainly, anyone who wishes to learn these techniques will have a more willing partner, more frequent, satisfying sex, and will also find natural protection from pregnancy and sexually transmitted diseases.

Other possible advantages of Effective Touching.

Some women might argue, "But if men please women so effectively that we want sex as much as men, what power will we have? The ability to withhold sex from a man, in a male-dominated society, is our only weapon. Now you want to take this away also?"

Such a question might emerge from one entrenched in a sexist culture, but again, a pleased woman becomes a willing partner. A man will not need to subjugate a passionately enthusiastic woman in order to get the sex he needs.

A willing partner!

James Cahill

How many men dream of this!
How many women dream of a patient and skilled lover!

Imagine, if we loved with equity in our pleasure, and participated frequently and generously in this wonderful, natural activity that is our birthright, a true gift to us all. How would our relationships change? How does the dynamic of this very private act underpin the way we arrange entire cultures? What if all men learned how to effectively please their women? Would the entire world shift a bit, righting itself on its axis ever so slightly?

Of course, manliness in many cultures is determined by the number of women a man penetrates and the number of children he has. And many women are conditioned to believe in feminine subservience. There are many deeply entrenched attitudes that might take a long time to shift, if ever.

To shift the definition of manliness from penetrating lots of women (or 'racking up numbers') to 'giving one woman incredible pleasure' would certainly be an approach, but this may sound like blasphemy in some cultures. However, people can change. In Uganda, they commendably cut their HIV rate in half by encouraging condoms and monogamy. In America, gays and lesbians are exiting the closet and becoming mainstream. Such behavior was very recently considered a moral abomination and a mental illness. We should not be so intimidated by entrenched ideas. Attitudes and traditions are dynamic and fluid. Is it truly so hard to imagine a man sitting at a bar, boasting, not about how many women he nailed, but rather, about how many orgasms he gave his wife in just this past week?

When sex works, as Mariah the therapist says, this fact alone might be enough to hold a marriage together. In a country where our divorce rate hovers above fifty percent, what a boon this would be to families and particularly to children. And is it crazy to speculate: how much of the nightmarish sex-trafficking industry would diminish if wives were more enthusiastic about sex?

This question of changing long held attitudes, of course, begs the thorny question of female circumcision. This tradition has been around for thousands of years, and is so deeply entrenched that it may very well persist for thousands more. But if its purpose is truly to keep women faithful, wouldn't teaching men about a clitoris and what to do with it serve the same goal more effectively?

The beneficial possibilities of effective lovemaking are numerous and significant, and certainly, the immediately tangible benefits like preventing unwanted pregnancies should be part of a many-pronged approach to solving larger problems. This is simply asking that we consider a new way of thinking about our sexual selves, the opposite sex, and learn a few techniques that will increase our joy in life and lovemaking tremendously. *Imagine*, to borrow again from the great John Lennon, a world where men and women please each other with skill, empathy, frequency and gusto. Is it presumptuous to think that such a shift in behavior might effect some larger, global changes? Hard to say, but let's begin simply, by making changes in our own lives. If we can each create a shift in our own tiny corner of the universe, well, who can tell where it all might lead.

www.ingramcontent.com/pod-product-compliance
Lightning Source LLC
Chambersburg PA
CBHW062317290526
45794CB00005B/1828